Saltwell Park

The story of the 'People's Park'

The Swings, Saltwell Park, Gateshead.   2689

by Anthea Lang

Introduction

Saltwell Park is regarded as one of the finest public parks in Great Britain and the best municipal park in the North East. Grade II listed by English Heritage, it contains 12 Grade II listed buildings, chief of which is the fairytale castle which we know today as Saltwell Towers. A £10 million restoration, funded by Gateshead Council and the Heritage Lottery Fund was completed in 2005, and in the same year the park was voted Britain's best park.

For nearly 140 years, many people in and around Gateshead have visited the park which has seen new features added (and often subsequently removed) in line with changing needs and fashions.

With this book, I hope to extend people's knowledge about the park and perhaps prompt people to remember some of the park's now forgotten features.

I would like to dedicate this book to all the many gardeners and Park Superintendents who have worked so hard over the years to give us this lovely green space – the 'green lung' of Victorian Gateshead.

Anthea Lang
May 2013

Acknowledgements

Many people have helped with information and reminiscences but among them are Roger Fern, Mary Richardson, Brenda Simm, Doug Clayton, Friends of Saltwell Park, Stuart Frazer, Michael Scott, Helen Ward and Michael Turner. As ever, thanks are due to staff of Tyne & Wear Archives & Museums and staff of Gateshead Central Library. And of course to my publisher, Andrew Clark, without whose help this book might never have seen the light of day.

East side of the lake in the 1920s.

Front cover: This photogenic little girl was probably placed in position by the postcard photographer. Perhaps she was his daughter? Photographs c 1913.

First published in 2013 by

Summerhill Books
PO Box 1210, Newcastle-upon-Tyne NE99 4AH

www.summerhillbooks.co.uk

Email: summerhillbooks@yahoo.co.uk

ISBN: 978-1-906721-65-7

Background

Gateshead, for much of the nineteenth century, was not a pleasant place to live in. The population was continually increasing (between 1841-71 it rose by almost 50%), and the bulk of this was crammed into tenements on Gateshead's quayside and in ramshackle courts and entries running off Bottle Bank and the High Street. Three cholera epidemics together with outbreaks of typhus (the 'Irish fever'), scarlet fever and other infectious diseases provided plentiful proof of the unsanitary conditions in which most people were living.

Heavy industries and a variety of noxious trades meant pollution on a large scale, whilst the infrequent fresh water supply posed a very real health problem. Yet there was some hope. Gradually, as the century wore on, Gateshead saw a gradual expansion of available building land as the moneyed industrialists who, earlier in the century, had bought huge swathes of land on which they typically built a house, lodge and stables, now began to see that profits could be made by selling their surplus acres to speculative builders.

One such industrialist was William Wailes, one of the country's leading stained glass window manufacturers who, in 1853, had purchased the bulk of an area known as the Saltwell Cottage Estate. But Wailes was not to sell his estate to a speculative builder. Instead, he sold his land and everything on it, including his house, to Gateshead Corporation to use as a public park.

Right: The only portrait of Wailes known to exist. Artist Francis Oliphant.

MANSION HOUSE AND LAND,
IN THE BOROUGH OF GATESHEAD.

TO BE SOLD BY PUBLIC AUCTION, at the Grey Horse Inn, in Gateshead, on TUESDAY, the Eleventh day of January, 1853, at One for Two o'clock in the Afternoon, (unless previously disposed of by Private Sale,)

MR. CHARLES BROUGH, AUCTIONEER, All that excellent MANSION HOUSE, with the Stables and Outbuildings attached, called SALTWELL COTTAGE, situate within a mile and a half of the towns of Gateshead and Newcastle, together with the Garden, Lawn, and LAND adjoining, the total contents (including the Sites of the Buildings) being 18A. 1R. 35P., or thereabouts.

The House is a modern erection—well arranged—possessing every requisite convenience — and commanding an uninterrupted view of the Vale of Tyne, and the Castle and Park of Ravensworth. The Stables and Outbuildings have been recently erected on the most improved principles, without regard to cost, and contain stall accommodation for upwards of sixty horses, together with loose boxes and carriage houses. The Land is in pasture of the richest character; and the whole Estate presents an opportunity rarely to be met with for the Establishment of a Horsedealer—the late Owner having carried on that Business extensively for the last thirty years.

As a Residence for a Gentleman possessing a large Stud, the property also presents peculiar attractions. From its vicinity to the town of Newcastle the property might also be advantageously occupied as a small Dairy Farm. The intended Line of the Team Valley Railway passes through the property.

The Property will be sold subject to such Conditions as will be produced at the time of Sale.

For further particulars, apply to Mr. EDWARD N. GRACE, Byker; Mr. JOSEPH ROBSON, Gateshead; Messrs. KELL & APEDAILE, or Mr. J. W. SWINBURNE, Solicitors, Gateshead.

How the estate was advertised on 8 January 1853 in the Gateshead Observer. (The house referred to here was not Saltwell Towers.)

Public parks were seen as one way in which the health of the nation could be improved. They provided large spaces, often referred to as an 'oasis of green', where rich and poor could mingle, allow the populace to breathe clean air and of course, provide a lure away from the public house, at a time when drunkenness was regarded as a serious social evil. Another attraction was that they were free. Public Health Acts of 1848 and 1875 allowed Councils to buy or lease land to be used *"for public walks or pleasure grounds"* and provided a major impetus to the rise of the public park in this country.

Gateshead already had a public park on Windmill Hills but, incapable of expansion, it was too small to be effective. The newly formed Park Committee of 1874 were faced with the dilemma of finding a new site large enough for development.

At first, the favoured area was at Shipcote, where Sir Walter James (later to be Lord Northbourne) was willing to sell about 40 acres, which the Gateshead Observer reported *"could be converted into a very nice park, which would be the means of attracting the working man in the borough to enjoy the beauties of the place and allure [sic] them away from many of the temptations now so prevalent in their midst ... its elevated position will enable the spectators on a clear day to have a grand view of Durham Cathedral".*

The only problem was the price. Sir Walter was asking £650 per acre – an amount so high that the Town Clerk wrote a letter on

1 October 1874 saying *"the Committee think there must be some mistake as the price asked for the 15 acres is more per acre than has been asked from other parties for building purposes".* (The 15 acres referred to was a specific piece of prime building land.)

But there was no mistake. The matter of the park was discussed at a public meeting on 6 October and when the price was revealed, the language became heated. William Wailes' estate was then mentioned as a possible alternative to Sir Walter's and eventually, after some debate, the motion carried was *"That as desirable sites are for sale, this meeting urges upon the Town Council the importance of negotiating to secure a site on the best possible terms".* Sir Walter, distinctly unamused at the language used at this meeting, speedily withdrew his offer of land. A letter in the Gateshead Observer of 10 October 1874, signed by *"An old inhabitant"* urged the Council to buy Wailes' estate. He suggested that Mr Wailes' land might be suitable as *"his grounds ... were I believe, laid out by one of the most eminent landscape gardeners* [Edward Kemp] *in the country".*

For many reasons, this proved to be a more than sensible alternative.

Wailes seems to have begun planting his estate shortly after he purchased it. The northern section consisted of four fields which were separated from another expanse of green by a natural dene. Within two years of his purchase, he had planted up the dene, constructed meandering paths and little bridges over the streams, and formed a driveway with access to roads at both the eastern and western edges of the estate. Outer plain walls with an inner castellated belvedere wall followed and then finally by 1871 the house, which we know today as Saltwell Towers, was built. Around his house, Wailes created well defined and differently styled areas which included a geometrical garden and an arboretum.

Wailes seems to have been heavily involved in the designs for both his house and his gardens but certainly, so far as his landscaping was concerned, he had help from one of the most important garden designers of the nineteenth century – Edward Kemp – a man who would eventually be responsible for the major part of the park's design. In fact, Kemp had referred to Wailes in his book on garden design 'How to layout a garden' published in 1858. Kemp wrote *"Such a* [rose] *walk I remember to have designed for William Wailes Esq., of Saltwell near Gateshead, where regular oblong beds were cut out in a band of grass on either side of the walk ... The walk itself, along the front of the kitchen garden ... was entered through a wire arch mantled with climbing roses".*

While all this work was progressing, Wailes was living at South Dene Towers (the crematorium is now on the site) and possibly also other houses in the vicinity. He later sold off South Dene and an area known as the Far Nancy Pit Field on which Ashfield House was later built.

Left: South Dene Towers in 1865 – the year Wailes sold this house to John Marriner Redmayne, a chemical manufacturer for £12,500.

In 1872, the Salte Welle was constructed and two years later, Wailes was seriously considering selling off his northern fields for building purposes. However, when he heard that negotiations with Sir Walter James had come to an abrupt halt, he began negotiations with the Council and offered them various options of land to buy for use as a public park.

Wailes' eponymous 'Salte Welle' built in 1872, complete with its gothicised inscription, drinking trough and a smaller trough underneath inscribed "for ye goode of thirstie dogges".

In March 1875, Wailes wrote a long letter to the Park Committee setting out these options in detail, ending *"I trust the above may not only be satisfactory but intelligable [sic]"*.

The Park Committee, carefully considering the financial situation of Gateshead's residents, then recommended purchasing the dene and as much of the four fields as could be obtained for an annual 3d rate saying that *"we would have been very glad to recommend the purchase of the entire property and have only refrained from doing so lest the burden of taxation upon the Borough should become excessive"*.

However, it was eventually decided that before proceeding, it would be a good idea to see how much money they were likely to get through a loan from the Local Government Board and with this in mind, a deputation of six local MPs, together with the Mayor and Town Clerk of Gateshead, proceeded to London to put their case. They proposed to *"purchase the whole of the Saltwell Estate with the Mansion House and other erections shown belonging to William Wailes ... containing a superficial area of 52 acres at the price of £32,000 ... [The park] is very advantageously situated and is easily and readily approached from every part of the Borough"*.

They also applied for a further £3,000 to cover the costs of laying out the park. The loan was agreed and on 6 February 1876, William Wailes received £12,000 cash – the first instalment of his payment. A further four years would elapse before the final conveyance and final payment was made but in the meantime, Wailes was a happy man. He had become a tenant in his own house paying an annual rent of £120, and had a substantial sum of money in the bank.

The scene was now set for the development of what would, in a very short space of time, become known as 'The People's Park'.

Right: The only SP (Saltwell Park) grate remaining in the park is situated at the base of the Salte Welle.

Beginnings of the Park

The park was being planned some months before all the financial arrangements were finalised and in November 1875, Gateshead Council asked John Hancock, the noted Newcastle naturalist, to provide a design. However, he declined, which meant that the Town Clerk had to inform the Park Committee that *"John Hancock would not be preparing a competitive plan as he was engaged in other work"*.

It seems to have been William Wailes who then suggested his former landscape designer, Edward Kemp, to the Committee. This was a wise move. Not only did Kemp know the estate but he was the Park Superintendent at Birkenhead, England's first public park, where he had worked with Joseph Paxton (designer of the Crystal Palace). Kemp charged four guineas (£4.20) per day plus travelling expenses to create the park landscape.

The Council wasted no time. It was decided that *"Mr Wailes' gardener be instructed to employ six men to do what is necessary to maintain the park until Mr Kemp's plan is received"*. This was a reference to George Lindsay, who became the first Park Superintendent.

Kemp presented his first plan to the Council on 3 February 1876, (three days before Wailes had received his initial cash payment) with a second plan following on 12 April 1876, by which time a steam plough was already busily ploughing up the northern fields.

Also in April, Gateshead Council placed their first orders for the park. They ordered 62 wooden benches and one dozen metal plates bearing the words 'Please keep off the grass'. They also instructed that one policeman should be on duty at all times and that this should be increased to three on Sundays!

Kemp's estimates for laying out the park were submitted in May 1876. The final figure, excluding any buildings, came to £10,862 19s 9d (£10,862.98).

Saltwell Park opened to the public over the Whit weekend in May 1876. There was no formal opening and Kemp's planned features were still only on paper. Even so, the park was an immediate and early success and the Gateshead Observer proudly boasted that: *"Gateshead is now possessed of a park that is really worthy of the name ... It is to be hoped that it will have some effect in removing the unenviable notoriety that Gateshead, in common with other towns in the North of England, has attained for the intemperance and want of refinement of its people ... a portion of the estate is already beautifully laid out and ornamented and covered with a thick growth of trees and shrubs"*.

Kemp's optical illusion – the panorama stretched to Ravensworth.

Wailes had concentrated his efforts on the area around his house and the dene, creating a well thought out and varied landscape, perfect for a mansion in its own extensive grounds. However, the rest of his estate remained uncultivated. When planning the park, Edward Kemp had the challenge of creating a landscape for the whole of the park and designing features such as new paths and walkways which would lead people to explore the whole estate in a comfortable and uncrowded atmosphere. He had 52 acres in which to do it.

Kemp's second set of plans were displayed at the Town Hall in July 1876 and it was not long before there was pressure to start work on some of them. His ideas included widening the existing footpaths, creating a promenade walk and designing a main entrance at the north east corner of the park. This was sensible as not only was it close to where new housing, largely of Tyneside flats in a grid pattern, was being planned, but it also provided the visitor with a staggering panoramic view across the park and over to the Ravensworth estates, giving the illusion of vast swathes of greenery.

Kemp also provided for a bowling green, skating rink, croquet lawn, a lake of about three acres, a refreshment room and a site for a drinking fountain.

Although most of Kemp's ideas were adopted, his plans for iron railings around the park boundary resulted in *"Rather a lively discussion"* which took place at the Town Hall. Although this was supported by some Councillors, including Alderman Robert Stirling Newall (who lived at nearby Ferndene and over the next 20 years proved to be a source of some irritation to the Park Committee due to his frequent complaints), others, including the Mayor, thought this was mere extravagance. Eventually, a mix of both iron and wooden railings were added to the park. New entrance gates costing £29, displaying the then Gateshead Coat of Arms, were made by the Gateshead firm of Bainbridge and Crimson who would go on to produce more iron work in the park including the ornamental gates near the Salte Welle.

BAINBRIDGE & CRIMSON,

Ironfounders, Smiths & Bellhangers.

| SOLE AGENTS FOR JOAL & CO.'S ELECTRIC and PNEUMATIC HOUSE BELLS. | STABLE FITTINGS. ROOFING, TYE RODS, &c. WROUGHT OR CAST IRON GIRDERS. RAILING AND ENTRANCE GATES. RAIN-WATER GOODS.   CISTERNS. SHOP SHUTTER GEARING. FITTINGS. | HOT WATER ENGINEERS, &c. |

ESTIMATES FOR ANY OF THE ABOVE MAY BE HAD ON APPLICATION.

2, Oakwell Gate (NEAR THE BATHS), GATESHEAD.

An advert for Bainbridge & Crimson of Oakwellgate, Gateshead.

Entrance gate Coat of Arms – A little reminder of when the park opened.

Urinals and water closets were ordered in May and in July, the Borough Surveyor, James Bower, was instructed to provide a bandstand. On 31 March 1877, he was asked to prepare plans for a walk beside the bandstand with a rustic bridge 10 feet wide connecting it to the terrace walk near the house. (*See top photograph on front cover.*) He was also asked to prepare a plan for two shelter houses. He submitted his estimate of costs in June 1878 which included a refreshment house, gates, keepers lodge, extra planting and two shelter houses at a cost of £6,300.

By the end of 1878, a drinking fountain, the Broad Walk (Kemp's 'promenade'), a bowling green and a bandstand had been erected in the park. The paths were at first gravelled but later asphalted. People began to donate animals and birds to the park and flower planting had begun in earnest as described in the Gateshead Observer in February 1877, when it was noted that *"at least one mile of crocuses* [were] *peeping their heads up"*.

However, the Council were determined that all of Kemp's features should be added and, over the next twenty years, further applications for loans were made to the Board of Health. These were successful and provided money for two shelter houses, the lake, children's playground and a gymnasium. A refreshment house, further entrance gates and three lodges, together with provision of extra drainage and a second storey to the Park Superintendent's house were also provided. When members of the Board wanted to visit the park in 1888, the Council paid £16 4s 9d (£16.24) for a special tram to take them there.

Of course, people who came to the park were expected to conform to certain standards of behaviour and, to help with this, in 1881 the Town Clerk proposed a code of byelaws modelled on those in force at Newcastle's Leazes Park. It took some time before these eventually came into force, as the Local Government Board didn't like them, and they were returned in February 1882 *"greatly altered"*. In the meantime, handbills were displayed in and around the park, warning people against committing wilful damage and trespassing on the grass.

We don't know what the original opening hours were but they were probably similar to those in operation during 1881. These were extensive. In December, January and February, the park was open from 7am until 5pm, during March, April, September and October it opened from 6am-8pm and between May to August, the opening times were 6am-10pm. Certainly in the winter months, those visitors who arrived at the beginning and end of each day would have experienced the park in the dark.

The byelaws which eventually came into force contained some rather surprising clauses. Today, we might not think of taking our carpet to the park to give it a good clean, but beating your carpet or mat was forbidden, as was smoking anywhere other than on a specific 'smoking' bench.

One of the very early 'unofficial' regulations, banned wheeled vehicles of any description. This included perambulators (prams) and resulted in numerous complaints including this letter which appeared anonymously in the Gateshead Observer for 3 June 1876:

"These vehicles of locomotion are allowed in the Newcastle parks and I have never heard that the privilege has been abused. I trust therefore that the authorities will reconsider the matter, put better faith in the matter and … admit the charmless things, which are the means of conveying little ones who are unable to walk at all, or so far, or who may be too heavy to be carried".

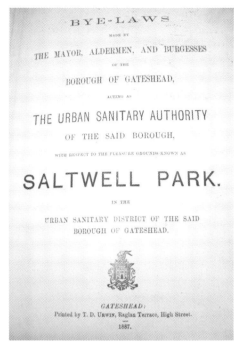

The cover of the 1887 byelaws.

Eventually, as can be seen from the photograph left, where at least three perambulators can be seen on the Broad Walk, the ban was lifted. Bicycles, however, were not allowed in the park until 1897 when it was agreed they could be wheeled through, but not ridden in, the park.

By now, the park was well established. New housing was providing a ready made local audience for events and a further impetus would come in 1909 with a new electric tram route direct to the park down Coatsworth Road and Brinkburn Avenue.

Left: Two views of the Broad Walk.

Top left: Looking north along the Broad Walk c 1925.

Bottom left: Looking south along the Broad Walk in the 1970s.

Early History of the Park

The park was soon a success, with the Northern Echo reporting in August 1889 that *"The public park at Saltwell is a great boon to the population after work hours"*. It became a centre for many of the important events held in Gateshead and some of the events held today, such as the Saltwell Show and the annual fireworks display, have their origins in these nineteenth century events. The Low Fell Floral and Poultry Society held their show in the park in 1881 and the flower show of the Gateshead Floral and Horticultural Society soon became an annual feature.

The first fireworks display was held in the park in August 1883, courtesy of Mr Paine of London (Paines were a well known fireworks company who also had a branch in the USA) who toured the country giving fireworks demonstrations. Profits were split two thirds to Paine and one third to the Council who made £97 7s 10d (£97.39). The Council were so pleased with these quick profits that they invited Paine back the following month. In 1884, he was back again, this time with an afternoon fete finishing with illuminations and a fireworks display. An admission fee of 6d (2.5p) was charged for adults while children were charged 3d. The workhouse children were given free admittance as a special treat.

However, not all requests were granted, as, for instance, in 1889, when both Mr Lowcraft of West Hartlepool who offered an aerial flight over the park, and Professor Baldwin who offered a balloon flight with a parachute descent by himself, were unsuccessful in their applications.

Sections of the park were often used for artillery drill but always on the condition that no damage was done. In 1888, the Town Clerk felt compelled to write to the Major in charge of the 5th Durham Rifle Volunteers complaining that they had occupied part of the park without permission and had brought horses into the park. The Town Clerk received an unqualified apology in return.

In 1883, over 1,000 people were entertained at a garden party held by the Mayor and Mayoress, Mr and Mrs William Affleck (Affleck was a builder who built many of Gateshead's terraces), and in September of the following year, 2,300 poor children of Gateshead were regaled with tea and buns through the kindness of the Mayor & Mayoress, Mr and Mrs Rankin.

However, these events pale into insignificance when compared with the festivities for Queen Victoria's Diamond Jubilee on 22 June 1897 when over 42,000 people piled into the park. 12,000 of these were children who assembled at their schools throughout Gateshead in the morning where they were each given a paper bag containing an orange and two buns and presented with a Jubilee medal in the form of a Maltese cross, with Queen Victoria's

22 June 1897 – Queen Victoria's Diamond Jubilee and crowds gather in the northern fields.

head on the obverse and the Gateshead Coat of Arms and the name of the Mayor, John Tulip Scott, together with the date of the Jubilee, on the reverse. Older pupils, some of whom had to walk considerable distances, marched in processions to the park where each school was allocated a special place on the northern fields, east of the bandstand. The local press reported in a somewhat ironic fashion *"When 12,000 children are gathered together in one limited space the sum of humanity which is represented strikes home with considerable force"*. The Mayor inaugurated the proceedings at 11.50 am and ten minutes later, at noon, the Union flag was hoisted and five bands performed the National Anthem. Half an hour later, the children were dismissed but two bands continued to entertain the adults until 2.45pm.

But even this event was surpassed fourteen years later, on what was described as *"a dull and gusty day"* when an estimated 50,000 people attended a fete on 22 June 1911 to celebrate the Coronation of

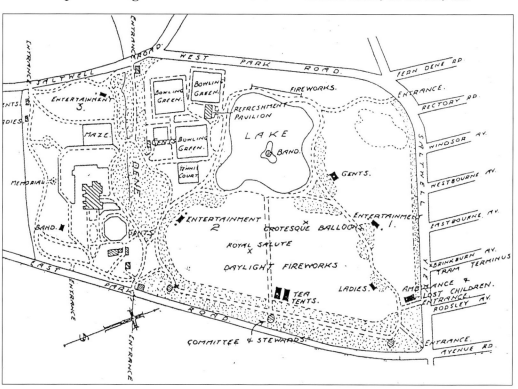

Map of the park produced for the celebrations of the Coronation of George V on 22 June 1911.

George V. The Mayor, Alderman John Costelloe, opened the proceedings and a Royal salute was fired. From 1.45pm until 10pm, sports were held in the playground, bands played and a performance was given by Mr Colin Veitch's concert party. The event was substantially funded by the Mayor who gave 100 guineas towards the cost. Unfortunately, medals, which were to be given to the children failed to arrive in time. Two English oaks, one for King George, the other for Queen Mary, were planted and grand floral displays were a feature along the Broad Walk.

Not all events, however, were so successful. In 1898, the Gateshead Floral and Horticultural Society had their rent waived due to wet weather, whilst forty years later, a week-long fete and pageant was similarly affected, only raising £50 instead of their estimated £1,000 for charity. A fireworks display, intended to close the event, had to be abandoned due to the bad weather.

Both the South African War (Boer War) and the First World War generated more solemn events in the park. In August 1901, about 20 men from the Gateshead contingent of Elswick Battery (1st Northumberland Volunteer Artillery) who had served in the Boer War were presented with silver medals, and four years later, in 1905, the memorial to the same war was unveiled.

Throughout the First World War, life continued in the park very much as it had prior to 1914, although the birds in the aviaries were reduced in number and the bowling greens were not so well tended as before the war. However, new boats were bought for the lake, new bowling equipment was purchased and the Park Committee continued to meet to discuss the weighty matters of who should be granted permission to hold events in the park. It is fair to say, that during the duration of

Souvenir Programme for the unveiling of the South African War memorial, 11 November 1905.

10

the war, the Committee were much more lenient in allowing events than they had been, and battalions and other organisations were frequently allowed the exclusive use of certain areas for drill practice and manoeuvres. The first anniversary of the declaration of war was held in the park on 4 August 1915. Various entertainments in aid of war related charities, such as the gala held by the Bowling Club in 1916 and the 1917 gymkhana, were also given. One successful event was the strawberry tea held by the Mayor, Ald William Wardill, in July 1916 in aid of 'Blind and Lame Soldiers and Sailors'. The Mayor was quoted as saying that it was: *"A success in every way"*.

During the war, visitors might have been surprised to see potatoes replacing the beautiful flower beds at the main entrance to the park. These were grown as part of the war effort and they did well – in one year, an initial purchase of 30 stones of seed potatoes for an outlay of £3, resulted in a yield of 427 stones of potatoes which sold for £23 15s (£23.75).

Saltwell Towers was converted into use as a V.A.D. (Voluntary Aid Detachment) military hospital, run jointly by the Red Cross and St John Ambulance Brigade, in 1916 and was a branch of a similar hospital at nearby Whinney House. Nine wards were created which could hold 50 beds. One of these beds was a gift of Newfoundland, whose premier, William Lloyd, had been born in Gateshead.

Town Hall,
Gateshead,
July 28th, 1915.

Dear Sir,

At the request of the Commanding Officer of the 68th Recruiting area, I have arranged to hold a Special Campaign in Gateshead, from August 2nd to 7th inclusive. I enclose Programme of Meetings and Processions.

May I ask for your kind and prompt co-operation in order that both Processions and Meetings may be as representative as possible.

I would especially call your attention to the meeting on the Anniversary of the Declaration Day, which will be held in Saltwell Park.

Yours faithfully,
W. E. WARDILL,
Mayor.

*Anniversary of Declaration Day,
4 August 1915.*

The £850 spent on medical and other equipment was largely raised by sales held by

Nursing staff and patients outside Saltwell Towers.

auctioneers and estate agents in the north east of England. The planned opening was scrapped as, due to heavy casualties on the Somme, patients were transferred to the hospital much earlier than expected. However, the building was eventually formally opened by the Mayor, William Wardill, on 22 July 1916. While the Towers was being used for this purpose, certain seats in the park were marked *"for the use of wounded soldiers only"*. Sir James Knott, the shipping magnate, presented two ambulances to the park to transport wounded soldiers to the hospital. These had been converted from cars which had formerly belonged to two of his sons, James and Basil, both of whom were killed during the war. After the war, the Council was presented with a certificate from the order of St John of Jerusalem – the only one granted to any corporation in the country – in gratitude for the use of the Towers.

A presentation to Sergeant Thomas Young of a watch, a silver cigarette case and some War Bonds, was made in the park on 30 June 1918, the day after Thomas had been awarded the Victoria Cross from George V. Thomas Young, a young miner of High Spen, served as a stretcher bearer during the war with the 9th Battalion of the Durham Light Infantry (DLI). He was awarded the VC as, on nine separate occasions, he had gone into No Man's Land (the area between the British and German trenches) and searched for wounded soldiers whom he then brought back to camp, often having first dressed their wounds, sometimes under heavy gun fire. At the ceremony he gave a short speech:

"I am not much of a speaker. There's not a man of the Durhams who wouldn't have done what I did: it was just what any one of them would have done if he could. The thing happened to come my way and I did it. That's all."

On 4 August 1918, the fourth anniversary of the outbreak of the war, a day of remembrance was held in the park, presided over by the Mayor of Gateshead, John Maccoy (who had himself lost a son in the war). The following year, Peace Day, 19 July 1919, saw a victory march from the Town Hall ending in the park where entertainment, including a temporary cinema and a fireworks display, was held.

One new feature which appeared in the park in 1903 was the 'penny in the slot' automatic weighing machine on the Broad Walk, outside the Almond Pavilion. Other new features included three bowling pavilions, two tennis courts, a paddling pool, a rose garden and an extension to the park in the form of Saltwell Grove estate. And, after a long period of unoccupancy, the mansion house was converted to a museum.

Thomas Young VC of High Spen.

On 5 September 1895, Eliezer Adler (considered the founder of the Jewish community in Gateshead) wrote to the Park Committee to ask for decorations from the park for the Jewish Tabernacle Feast (Sukkot). Unfortunately we don't know whether this request was granted but it demonstrates that the Jewish community were early users of the park.

Not all users, of course, behaved. Young men seem to have been a constant source of annoyance and in 1892 the sign 'For Ladies' began to appear on a number of seats in the park. This followed a number of complaints from ladies who could seldom get a seat in the park. Seats "... *were generally monopolised by young people, particularly young men, who sat, smoked and spat and would give way for nobody".*

The Broad Walk proved a great attraction to the young men. Unfortunately, however, in 1894, due to "... *the improper behaviour of young men occupying seats in the Park who by use of foul language and filthy remarks are a public disgrace, ladies especially being the butt of their coarse innuendoes and Sunday afternoon the time of their greatest activity",* two plain clothes policemen were employed in the park on Sundays *"to suppress the behaviour of half grown men who ... annoy females as they pass by".*

A solitary young lady outside the Almond Pavilion on the Broad Walk in the 1920s.

The Council were offered extra land on more than one occasion but usually declined as, in 1896, when Heathfield, a neighbouring estate to the east of the park, was offered for sale and again in 1902, when Lawrence Hill Armour, a Gateshead Alderman and architect, who designed many of the streets on the nearby Rodsley Estate, offered to sell a small portion of the Ferndene Estate.

However, one estate which *was* added to the park was the area known as Saltwell Grove. This five acre estate, which included a house of the same name (which remained outside the park), was bought in 1920 by the Council for £4,000 from the estate of Elisha Hunter Ryott. Once purchased, access to the Grove was simple – two archways were carved out in two places through the southern boundary wall which separated both estates (still the entrances today). The new extension opened on 12 May 1921, with a performance by the band of the Seaforth Highlanders and the Council took the opportunity to relocate the bandstand to the Grove from the lake where it had been since 1909. This was regarded as a popular decision, not least by the musicians who had had to be transported across the lake in order to perform. One thousand new chairs were ordered although early proposals to charge admittance to the Grove were never adopted.

By this time, of course, Gateshead's tram network had greatly improved and one of the services terminated at the end of Brinkburn Avenue, opposite the park. This meant it became easier for people from outlying districts to visit and a tram trip to the park was a popular activity. So popular in fact that, in 1938, so much congestion was caused by people waiting for trams and buses that two local residents offered to pay for three new seats at this entrance. The Council agreed and installed the seats but only after they had installed new gates, deliberately set back from the entrance, in another attempt to resolve the problem of congestion.

A tram on the way to the park, with the message 'Pay as you enter – have one penny ready'.

In 1935, the park was illuminated for the centenary of the Borough. More than a mile of multi-coloured lights were hung along the Broad Walk and down to the lake and members of St Mary's Church presented the 'St Mary's Pageant'.

The park was as popular with children as with adults and special 'children only' trams operated during school holidays. On Whit Monday, 1926, over 50 children were dealt with in the 'lost children' tent!

By 1939, the park's success was assured with the new features having only added to its attraction. However, the clouds of war were gathering and things were about to change.

Mayor, Coun Pickering with a crowd of children at the official opening of a charity fete held in the park in 1938.

Saltwell Park Ordnance Survey 4th edition 1939. This shows the park as it was just before the outbreak of the Second World War.

The Second World War

Saltwell Park really came into its own during the Second World War as a location for the Holidays at Home scheme which ran during the summers of 1942, 1943 and 1944. The scheme, scheduled across Britain for one week in June and another week in August, was designed to stop people travelling to far flung tourist spots, thus releasing pressure on the overloaded railway system. Gateshead's programme placed emphasis on activities for the local children including boating, donkey and pony rides, Punch and Judy shows and foot races. For adults, water polo matches, tetherball games and bathing beauty and dance contests together with bowls tournaments and dancing were held although dancing to the band of the Durham Light Infantry and jitterbugging on grass must have been rather more difficult than on a conventional dance floor. Roundabouts appeared but games of chance didn't, with one particular game, known as 'roll-em-in', being specifically banned.

The Minister of Labour says:
ENJOY YOUR
HOLIDAYS AT HOME
GET A BOOK FROM ONE OF
THE PUBLIC LIBRARIES
AND READ IT IN
BEAUTIFUL
SALTWELL PARK

Forget the war – read a book!

As well as Holidays at Home, there were other events. On 25 September 1940, a band concert was held by Ravensworth Collieries Prize Band to raise money in aid of the Mayor of Gateshead's Spitfire fund. A Wings for Victory week was held in the park during June 1943 (*see page 16*) and on 15 May 1945, a Thanksgiving Parade was held in the Park.

But the park was not simply used for pleasure in war time. It had other far more practical uses. Opposite Saltwell View, a large underground air raid shelter was dug in a section of the playground. This could hold 648 people – many residents close to the park lived in Tyneside flats and would simply not have had space to erect their own shelters. As access to the shelter was needed at all times, the three entrance gates on the north side of the park remained unlocked throughout the duration of the war.

The shelter, however, was little used as Gateshead remained virtually 'bomb free' throughout the Second World War. However, on the night of 3/4 May 1941, a stick of bombs was dropped on the park which blew out some of the windows in the houses opposite and damaged the doors of the newly constructed Little Theatre. Tram poles outside the park were also damaged.

DANCING ON THE GREEN
EVERY MONDAY, THURSDAY and SATURDAY
In the Playground, Saltwell Park
FROM
JULY 27th to AUGUST 22nd

For Times, Bands, and other Particulars see Official Programmes, Price ONE PENNY, on sale at the Public Libraries, Saltwell Park, Swimming Bath, and Shipley Art Gallery.

Enjoy a dance in the park.

HOLIDAYS AT HOME BOOKS
(mostly short stories)
are provided by the Gateshead Public Libraries Committee.

Get one from the Park Attendant and read it in these beautiful surroundings.

Before leaving the Park return it to the attendant or deposit it in the box.

It didn't matter if you forgot to return these books as they had already been withdrawn from stock!

A Spitfire proudly displaying Gateshead's Coat of Arms.

As in the First World War, the park was also used for training exercises and manoeuvres and exercises were held for the Local Defence Volunteers, precursors of the Home Guard.

Some of the park buildings were given extra functions during the war. The bandstand and the shelter in the Grove were both approved by the Ministry of Food as sites for airing gas contaminated foodstuffs, while the Indo-Chinese Pavilion was transformed into a British restaurant in 1943. These restaurants provided food for people who had run out of food rationing coupons.

During the first year of the war, some of the park's railings were removed for the war effort – a ruling which was flawed, as most cast iron railings were unsuitable for war purposes anyway. Not all were removed however, as it was revealed that the initiative did not apply if the railings were needed for boundary purposes.

Allotments also appeared in the park during the war with allotment holders being provided with plants from the Park Superintendent. In 1939 it had been decided that these would be situated in the old playground area in the north west of the park and one plot was designated as a demonstration allotment.

Building operations for the air raid shelter.

However, this particular allotment was only in place for one year as it was often subjected to thefts of vegetables and damage was frequently caused. Further allotments were created in 1942 in the adjoining area, damaged by the bomb explosion of the previous year.

Vegetables grown in the park were supplied in the first instance to the British restaurants at wholesale prices although potatoes and tomatoes grown in the park were given first to hospitals and institutions in Gateshead.

The allotments were not the only sites of criminal activities however, as, in 1942, two blankets were stolen from the ambulance hut and in 1943, damage to trees and shrubs in the Dene was blamed on the large number of children and youths who frequented the park on Sunday afternoons.

Servicemen got some park 'perks' during the war. In 1940, it was decided that troops stationed in Gateshead were allowed the free use of a bowling green so long as they were in uniform and wore suitable sandshoes or overshoes. There was some relaxation of the rules for games and sports in the park as for example with skating which was allowed to take place on Sundays.

Not all news stories could be reported at the time but one which did make the local papers was the account of an auction held in the park in June 1943 when Lance Bombardier Smith brought home from Gibraltar a banana and a lemon and auctioned both, with the proceeds going to the RAF Benevolent Fund. The banana raised £5 1s (£5.05) while the lemon was purchased for a staggering £8!

A salutary reminder of the war came during lake dredging operations in 1996 when a two pound Second World War anti-tank shell was found in the lake. Army experts were called from Catterick and the offending item removed.

COUNTY BOROUGH OF GATESHEAD.

WAR-TIME ALLOTMENTS

Plots are available in various parts of the town for allotments. Applications invited— Rent 5/- per annum. For further information apply to Town Clerk.

ENFIELD,
Durham Road,
GATESHEAD, 9.

Dig for Victory

Wings for Victory

Decline and Restoration

After the war, life in the park continued very much as it had done prior to 1939. This period however, whilst it saw the arrival (and demise) of some new features such as the sensory garden, the 'Cube' and the George Wilkes Bowling Pavilion, also saw the removal of the bandstand, the paddling pool, the Indo-Chinese Pavilion and the closure of the museum. There was no doubt however, that the wartime Holidays at Home scheme had an influence on the type of events held in the park in the years immediately following. Pony rides were held in the park during 1947 and in the same year, sheep dog trials were held. These were initially very successful. Shepherds, with their dogs, visited from the south of Scotland, Northumberland, Durham and Yorkshire and it was recorded that *"marvellous displays of intelligence, patience, obedience and delightful 'style'"* were to be seen. These were not however obvious on the occasion at the 1948 show, when a lone sheep, separated from its companions by the sheepdog, caused chaos when it bolted towards the Mayor and the rest of the Civic party, leapt a hedge and landed in a flower bed! However, as people gradually realised that it was perfectly possible to watch the trials without paying to go into the special enclosure, the shows began to make a loss and were eventually discontinued in 1958.

The 'Mary Adelaide' model train was a feature in the park for a few years from 1947. It could carry up to 40 children for 3d (2p) each and ran on a track roughly 200 metres in circumference. No one could accuse this train of being uneconomical to run – for every four hours of running, it only needed two dustpanfuls of anthracite.

County Borough of Gateshead

SALTWELL PARK
SPECIAL ATTRACTION

SHEEP DOG TRIALS

Saturday, 28th June

Official Opening by His Worship The Mayor.
(Ald. N. McCretton) at **2.15 p.m.**

The Competitors for the Gateshead Challenge Cup and Medal will include Shepherds from the South of Scotland, Northumberland, Durham and Yorkshire, and many famous dogs will appear.

Marvellous displays of intelligence, patience, obedience and delightful "style"

Arranged by Adam Telfer, Esq., of Cambo, Morpeth

ADMISSION TO GROUND FREE.   ENCLOSURE SEAT 1/-

An advert for the sheepdog trials in 1947.

The 1953 Coronation saw another fireworks display in the park which was illuminated for the occasion (*below*). 1953 also saw a storm of protest from the Lord's Day Observance Society when they realised that, for the first time, Saltwell Flower Show would be open on a

Sunday. Their protest however, fell on deaf ears and the Sunday opening remained.

The war time allotments were removed in 1955 and the following year, the sensory garden, an enclosed area with raised, highly scented bedding, was created to the east of the South African War Memorial.

In 1956, a Modern Homes & Trades Exhibition (*see right*) was held, with over 60 stands showing a variety of labour saving gadgets, fireplaces and children's pets. Shephard's store gave fashion shows four times daily, pony rides were available and 50 people were enrolled as new donors for the blood transfusion service. Unfortunately, the Exhibition was doomed by the weather when 70mph winds resulted in havoc and two marquees were destroyed.

Other annual events which appeared during this period included the North of England Rose, Carnation and Sweet Pea Society (Rosecarpe) from the 1960s whilst the 1970s saw the start of 'Wor Day', a Council initiative with entertainment and floats provided from various local organisations.

Modern Homes & Trades Exhibition, 1956.

A ripple of unease ran through the park in 1973 when plans were unveiled for a new motorway which would cut through the park. One hundred trees were threatened with destruction but thankfully these plans were eventually abandoned.

Mr Newsome's circus in 1886 started a long tradition of circuses coming to the park and they usually used the original playground site at the north west of the park. Later circuses included Barrett's Canadian Circus, who visited in 1950, Roberts Brother's Circus and the Circus Hoffman. This poster (*left*) advertises Circus Hoffman's visit in 1975. On that occasion they left so much litter behind that they were very nearly refused permission to return four years later.

Eventually, however, all circuses were banned from the park.

The 'Saltwell Airways' aeroplane was first seen in the park in 1982 and remained a feature until 1993. It had started life in 1953 as a V.701 series Viscount and flew for 20 years before being used for cabin crew training. It was then bought privately and was a feature of Lambton Lion Park. When this park closed, the plane was transferred to Saltwell Park. A staggering 22,299 people visited the plane in its first year in the park.

However, by the 1990s the park had become overgrown as saplings planted earlier in the century became large mature trees which at best partially masked, and at worst totally obliterated, Kemp's planned sightlines. Buildings such as the George Wilkes Bowling Pavilion and the stage-cum-kiosk were modern unattractive buildings which did not fit with the park's Victorian design. The Dene became overgrown and unsafe whilst Saltwell Towers, abandoned, unroofed and eventually railed off, presented all the appearance of Sleeping Beauty's castle.

Saltwell Airways.

Eventually in 1999 a successful bid was made to the Heritage Lottery Fund and a thorough restoration of both the park and Saltwell Towers was undertaken with the help of Gateshead Council. Completed in 2005, this resulted in two new play areas for different ages, improvements to the three bowling greens, the demolition of some of the more modern intrusive buildings, the conversion of the stable block to an education centre, plus restoration work to the aviaries, maze, rose garden and the lake. Saltwell Towers was rebuilt brick by brick, and transformed into an open plan café and gallery space.

But the story did not stop there and new features and events have continued. Since 1985, the park has been the setting for the annual Family Sculpture Day when families converge on the Grove area and produce amazing art work using a variety of materials and also, for a few nights in December, the 'Enchanted Parks' production which transforms the park into a winter wonderland of illuminated installations. Other annual features are the Cancer Relief fun run and Saltwell Harriers Road Race.

By the 1970s, trees had almost completely masked the Towers.

2010 saw the construction of the Tyne Bridge replica south west of the Towers. This was created for the 2010 Chelsea Flower Show where it won a bronze medal. Designed to commemorate the thirtieth anniversary of the Great North Run, flowers represent the runners who annually stream across the bridge. In July 2011, the friendship garden was unveiled celebrating 20 years of friendship between Gateshead and Komatsu in Japan. Ten gardeners from Komatsu city worked with council gardeners to create the garden which includes a stone pond and a waterfall where water is represented by gravel. This reciprocated the friendship garden which Gateshead had presented to Komatsu in 2001.

Above: The friendship garden.

Right: The replica of the Tyne Bridge.

Landscape Features

Saltwell Park has always been renowned for the quality of its floral displays. Flowers, trees and shrubs, always a feature of William Wailes' gardens in the grounds, continued to feature strongly in the newly created park with one of the first decisions of the Park Committee being to allocate funds for the provision of plants. One of the main purposes of the recent restoration scheme was to try to return the park to the way in which it would have looked in its early days with many of the overgrown plants, shrubs and trees being cut back or removed altogether. The Dene was one of the main focal points of the scheme and one of the main successes as it was substantially improved from the derelict dumping ground it had become in the later years of the twentieth century.

The Dene.

When the park first opened, planting was largely confined to the area around the mansion house. To the south of the house, Wailes had created a naturalistic landscape typical of Lancelot 'Capability' Brown (one of the most noted landscape designers of the eighteenth century), separated from his other more cultivated gardens by a ha-ha (a turfed ditch used in landscapes to prevent animals from accessing lawned areas) and a belvedere wall with mock fortifications. To the west was his sunken garden while the Dene lay north of his house and his 'geometrical' garden (later to become the octagonal bowling green) was to the east of the house. This meant that whichever window Wailes looked from, he had a very different landscape to view.

Gardeners on the Broad Walk.

Wailes' gardener, George Lindsay, became the Council's first Park Superintendent, and, together with Robert Stirling Newall's gardener, he selected the first plants specifically for the park. A well known firm of seedsmen, Stuart and Mein of Kelso, were awarded the first contract to supply plants in February 1877, and over the next few years annual sums of money were allocated for further plants. Propagating houses were erected and the displays of Victorian 'carpet bedding' became celebrated.

Whilst most people appreciated the beautiful floral displays which became such a feature of the park, one of the first recorded crimes in the park took place in March 1877 when flowers were stolen from the Dene and seats and trees were defaced. Other 'criminals' were the ever increasing collection of rabbits which enjoyed eating the plants in the Dene to such an extent that the Council had to advertise for a rabbit catcher in 1931.

The Maze – bringing a whole new meaning to the phrase 'get lost!'

Most of Wailes' features were retained and improved within the park although, within 20 years, both of his ponds were converted to rockeries. The Maze he had planned for the younger members of his family, was completed in 1877. Always popular, it was replanted on a number of occasions although the yews, planted as part of the recent restoration programme, have now been replaced with a species of thuja.

The Dene, an existing natural feature, was laid out by Wailes to resemble a Scottish glen. However, Kemp changed this to give it a more Italianate appearance, adding pools and waterfalls.

A number of bridges crossed the Dene – the highest was a stone bridge, which was used as a carriageway with other shorter wooden bridges acting as footpaths. All these bridges suffered from problems over the years (a horse managed to put its foot through the planks of one in 1887) and were frequently rebuilt.

One bridge which never appeared in the Dene however, was the medieval stone bridge over the river Team which was being dismantled in 1883. W.H.D. Longstaffe, a noted antiquarian, suggested that this be rebuilt in the Dene. Although the Council liked the idea of having a historic bridge in Saltwell Park, they were unwilling to allocate the £115 estimated to move and rebuild it; consequently, the proposal was not adopted and the bridge was demolished.

One of the original wooden footbridges over the Dene.

As part of the recent restoration, the bridges were rebuilt, the stream course in the Dene was re-aligned and a pumping system was provided to re-circulate the water.

Mr Wilson (seated centre) – the park's head gardener with his daughter Alice Smith (in white blouse).

Other early landscape features were shown in Kemp's plans but the designs were executed, sometimes amended, and overseen by James Bower, the Borough Surveyor. The Broad Walk, a Kemp feature, was laid out and planted in February 1877 and the local press noted *"It will become one of the finest promenades in the country"*. The Broad Walk soon became the fashionable place in the park in which to walk and also, incidentally, it provided a good location for courtship activities. Walks like these were devices commonly used by many of the early park designers, men such as J.C. Loudon and Joseph Paxton, whose ideas Kemp adopted. The Broad Walk, was, and still is, divided from the adjoining fields. At first, it was separated by wooden hurdles but these were later replaced by hedging. This acted as a deterrent to the sheep which often grazed on the fields in the park's early years and which might otherwise have paid unwelcome attentions to the young ladies parading in all their finery along Kemp's promenade.

Footbridges, one wood, one of stone, were used to bridge Wailes' ha-ha. The bridge shown on the cover cost £21 12s (£21.60) when it was built in 1913.

The Grove area of the park, opened in 1921, was improved ten years later when old walls were demolished and the present shelter houses

The Grove, Saltwell Park, Gateshead. 3940

were built along the north wall. New rockeries were also added and the drains improved. However, access to Saltwell Grove House (not part of the park) was comparatively still easy as can be seen in this photograph (*above*) and there were numerous accounts of children

The rose garden, c 1950. When this opened, 3,500 rose bushes were planted!

climbing the railings and stealing plants from the house's private gardens.

The Rose Garden was begun in 1935 on what had originally been William Wailes' kitchen garden which had later been used as nurseries. Angus McBean, the then Park Superintendent, designed it as a project for unemployed men. This was a very successful scheme and it opened in July 1936.

The Sensory Garden was constructed in 1956 to the south east of the Towers and had raised flower beds and scented flowers labelled in braille. Unfortunately, certainly in its early days, this proved more popular with courting couples and Alderman Norman McCretton complained that the area was being used for canoodling. He added *"It is the seclusion and romantic smell which attracts the lovers – but now we're going after them"*. What the result of this was, we don't know!

Trees have always been a notable feature in the park and many have been planted to commemorate Royal events such as coronations and jubilees. On the first occasion this happened, for Queen Victoria's Diamond Jubilee, things, apparently, did not quite go to plan. £20 was set aside for trees and it was agreed that 60 children would each plant a tree along the West Park Road boundary of the park. Each child received a certificate. However, having started at the Dene, they had only managed to fit in half that number by the time they reached the main gates at Saltwell View.

In 1911, to celebrate the coronation of George V, the Mayoress, Mrs Costelloe, and the Town Clerk's wife, Mrs Swinburne, planted English oaks near the main

Araucaria araucana (Monkey Puzzle tree) today.

entrance to the park. A tree planting with a rather more sober and poignant message was the oak tree from Verdun (one of the most devastating battles of the First World War) planted on Peace Day in 1919 by the Mayoress, Miss Daisy Maccoy.

The photograph below shows the Mayoress, Mrs Mary Armstrong, planting a tree on the

occasion of George V's Silver Jubilee in 1935 near the south end of the Broad Walk. Two oak trees were planted in 1953 to celebrate Queen Elizabeth II's Coronation while Walter Gore, the Artistic Director to the London Ballet, presented six flowering chestnuts in April 1964 which were planted as a group on one of the lawns adjoining the maze.

Left: The Mayor, Timothy Armstrong, alongside the Deputy Mayor and the Town Clerk, watches his wife planting a ceremonial oak tree on the Broad Walk in 1935.

Some of the trees in the park are rare – in particular the fern-leaved beech, which may originally have been planted as a specimen tree in Wailes' landscape. There are a variety of other interesting trees in the park which range from a Monkey Puzzle tree (*see opposite page*), Chilean Pine, Blue Atlas Cedar and a yellow sycamore, to poplars and a yew, whose branches have been so misshapen by generations of children sitting on them that it is well nicknamed the 'octopus' tree.

As evening falls, people are still boating on the lake.

However, not all trees survive and, over the years, many have been cut down due to old age or disease. They have also been the subject of some criminal activities as in 1909 when the attention of the Watch Committee was called *"to the wanton destruction of trees at the park especially along the Saltwell View boundary"*.

The lake was part of Kemp's original plan, but was not constructed until 1880 at a cost of £542 3s 3d (£542.16). A number of people were involved in its creation – John Hancock designed a scheme for the planting around the lake edge and also proposed a beach for the east side of the lake (although this never

Catching tiddlers – always a popular pastime … but no railings!

seems to have happened), the town's surveyor James Bower designed the island and William Wailes provided a sketch for a rockery. When constructed, the size was four acres with a depth of four feet. Bower was faced with a number of problems regarding the lake. Like William Wailes' duck ponds, it leaked and Bower frequently asked for money to pay for extra water from the Water Company. Beside the lake, a paddling pool was created in 1925 which proved a very popular feature.

Due to reports of children falling in the lake, some attempt was made to provide railings around one particularly vulnerable section of the lake – an area where the footpath had a slope. However, there were still plenty of other parts of the lake which remained unprotected and many children over the years have had to walk home soaking wet!

Litter was an unfortunate feature in the park's early days, mainly due to the lack of litter bins. The park had been open for over 20 years before the first 'waste baskets' arrived in

1897. During the 1970s in an effort to combat a growing litter problem, bins in the shapes of fun animals were introduced. The current bins, introduced in 2002, were rather neatly designed as octagonal to match Kemp's original octagonal shaped features.

Kemp's landscape designs created a series of 'garden rooms' linked by large swathes of green which effectively gave the visitor to the park a series of ever changing views. No matter what buildings or other structures have been added to the park over the years, the basic plan has remained constant and contributed to the park's continuing success.

Left: One of today's litter bins.

Buildings in the Park

Saltwell Towers was at the centre of William Wailes' landscaped grounds and became the focal building in Kemp's Saltwell Park. Often referred to nowadays simply as 'the Towers', it was never called this originally, being referred to either as 'the mansion house' or 'Saltwell Dene House'. Over the years, it has seen a variety of uses and is currently used as the park's visitor centre and café. Despite numerous proposals to demolish it, the building has survived and its striking design makes it one of Gateshead's most outstanding buildings.

A humorous First World War photograph.

The architect of the house is unknown but the design may have been largely that of Wailes himself who had, apparently with his son, originally planned a quite different building when he first bought the estate. However, Wailes seems to have had a change of heart and pressed on in a style which was possibly influenced by building styles he had seen on previous continental tours, resulting in the Towers being built in a mix of English, Gothic and French styles. It was probably completed about 1871. Polychromatic bricks were used to great effect – this was a style Wailes had experienced in his previous residence South Dene Towers.

The large west facing bay windows of Wailes' master bedroom and the library underneath were deliberately designed to reveal spectacular panoramic views across the valley to the Ravensworth estate and the house was completed in grand style (*see opposite page*). Carvings on doors and panelling and much of the furniture were done by Gerrard Robinson (1832-91), one of the North East's premier woodcarvers of the nineteenth century, who also provided linen-fold panelling to many of the doors. The ornate ceilings, described as "*Splendidly moulded plaster*" contained bosses with shields bearing armorial designs. Every room, no matter how small, was designed in a highly decorative style.

The builder Wailes used, George Brown, was a jobbing builder, for whom this was probably his biggest project. Unfortunately, working to Wailes' idiosyncratic and fanciful design, he produced a building with more style than substance. The dramatic exterior masked what was essentially a flawed building, built without foundations, with only basic sanitation and a variety of badly linked roof levels and mis-matched guttering. Within twenty years, one of the ceilings had collapsed – the first in a long line of building problems.

Wailes died at Saltwell Towers in March 1881 by which time he had become the lessee of the house rather than the owner. Whilst Wailes might have been prepared to put up with the building problems, future tenants were not, and there were continuing complaints about the sanitation, the heating, and the inconvenient size of some of the larger rooms.

The first tenant after Wailes was Hugh Clayton Armstrong, a Newcastle timber merchant, while the second, from 1888 until his death in 1909, was Joseph Ainsley Davidson Shipley, a solicitor. He in turn was followed by James Rowell, a local brewer. Co-incidentally, Rowell, like Wailes before him, had also occupied South Dene Towers. All these tenants made certain demands of the Council before agreeing their tenancies – some of which had considerable

George Brown, the builder of Saltwell Towers.

effects on the park landscape and the interior of the house. It is perhaps a measure of the poor interior design and quality of the house that there was never any competition for each tenancy and virtually all demands were agreed to by the Council, who became increasingly desperate to stave off any potential periods of unoccupancy.

Armstrong's demands, in particular, had a direct influence on buildings in the park as he stipulated that he required a three stall stable, coach house and an entrance lodge and would be willing to pay 5% towards the costs. All of these were provided. In June 1886, Armstrong sent a letter to the Park Committee saying *"although the appearance of the house is good yet the accommodation is bad – the rooms are large and occupy more space than is necessary"*. This was probably an accurate statement – some years later the Council considered dividing the house into two – however, the relatively few numbers of rooms, their size and arrangement made this impractical and the idea was dropped.

The rooms with the views!

Armstrong surrendered his tenancy when the original five year lease was up and Shipley approached the Council with a view to leasing the Towers. His requests were to build an extension on the house in which to house his art collection and to remove the fireplace in the front room with one of his own choice. Both of these requests were agreed to although the extension was never built. Shipley could certainly have done with an extension as he was an avid collector of paintings and nine hundred and sixty seven of them were stored in the mansion house. In 1908, Shipley requested a telephone line and the Council agreed. They insisted, however, that the three telephone poles needed had to be carefully concealed behind trees.

Shipley died in 1909 and the following year the mansion was leased to John Henry Rowell, a local brewer, for five years for an annual rental of £120. Like Armstrong and Shipley before him, Rowell also had certain specific requests and one of these was to have electricity installed. This cost the Council £445 but they were so desperate to have the house occupied that they agreed.

The library with its elaborately carved furniture and bookshelves.

After Rowell died in August 1913, his widow kept the tenancy on until 1915 after which the house was used temporarily as a billet for soldiers and then, between 1916 and 1920, was used as an army hospital attached to the nearby Whinney House Hospital.

There was to be only one further tenant. This was Harold Svendsen, a garage owner, who moved into the house in 1920, again on a five year tenancy, but within two years had left, unable to pay the rent.

Attempts to lease the house following Mr Svendsen's departure were unsuccessful and the house remained unoccupied for over ten years – years which did nothing to improve its condition. This was a real problem so far as the Council was concerned and various uses were considered. Eventually, and after some debate, it was decided to turn the house into a museum.

The 'Local and Industrial Museum' was formally opened on 8 July 1933 by the Mayor, Ald J.H. Ritson, JP and used six of the building's twenty rooms. One room was designated for industrial science while another housed the local collection. The first curator was Frank Young, a noted naturalist. He was allowed to live in the house as a perk of the job.

The anticipated attendance was estimated at 3,000-4,000 per day and for a number of years, the museum remained a popular attraction. It was open until 8pm and it was a common sight to see queues of children. There was a wide range of exhibits although they concentrated on the Gateshead area. These included prints and engravings of Gateshead, the sign from the historic Goat Inn which had stood on Bottle Bank, portraits of local dignitaries, an umbrella stand reputedly made from wood of a mulberry tree sent from James I plus a 'quaint box' built of wood from one of the piles of the Roman Tyne Bridge. Also displayed were models of locomotives and ships and a variety of stuffed animals which were loaned by the Hancock Museum. Outside the entrance was a whale's jawbone, originally from the Sheriff Hill area of Gateshead.

In 1940, a very frail and ancient shop front was erected in the hall of the museum. The workmen had a harder job installing it than they anticipated and *"Much honest sweat was expended in the removal of the ancient putty, which was of a rock-like consistency"*. In the same year, the Dodds sisters, (founders of the Little Theatre opposite the park) provided a Victorian room complete with furnishings in memory of their aunts the Misses Mawson of nearby Ashfield.

The museum continued to be an attraction until the late 1960s when the perilous condition of the building finally made itself known, and the floorboards gave way. The building was closed on 12 February 1969, with most of the exhibits being hastily removed to the Shipley

The shop front which was installed in the Museum in 1940.

Items for sale – at 1900 prices!

Gallery. For the next 30 years, the Towers became the centre of controversy over its eventual conservation or demolition. Within a year of closure, a 'Save the Museum Fund' had been established but sadly, although there were numerous donations from organisations such as the Little Theatre, Fenwicks and Littlewoods stores, it was not enough, and Tyne & Wear County Council were asked to take the Towers for use as a museum. Unfortunately, the cost of this restoration was prohibitive and they refused.

A proposal in 1971 to turn the Towers into a planned ruin was shelved and to the Council's dismay, the Department of the Environment placed a preservation order on the building and gave it a Grade II listing. This meant it could not be demolished but the Council lacked the money necessary to carry out repairs. A later appeal against the ruling was lost and so in 1985, the building was simply railed off and remained looking like Sleeping Beauty's fairytale castle until restoration began thanks largely to a

The Victorian room, in memory of the Misses Mawson of Ashfield House.

Heritage Lottery Grant in 1998. By then, a tree could be seen growing out of the tower!

The only other building structure remaining today which was the responsibility of William Wailes was the Salte Welle, which he restored in 1872 and from which the park gets its name. Wailes originally sited this on the boundary wall of the park facing Saltwell Lane. However, when the lane was relaid and raised (now Saltwell Road South), the well ended up facing a wall – not quite so picturesque.

The main inscription, complete with spelling mistake (possibly deliberate as a piece of pseudo-medievalism) says: *"Whosoever drynketh of this water shall*

The Salte Welle on Saltwell lane with the new road under construction in the late 1920s.

thriste [sic] *agayne. But whosoever drynketh of the water that CHRIST shall give him shall never be more a thirste but the water He shall give him shallbee in him a welle of water springing up with everlastynge lyfe".* [John 4:14] However, if you look carefully at the base of the well a small archway has the lettering *"for ye goode* [sic] *of thirstie dogges".*

The well was restored in March 1953 when it was described as *"ready to give its healing waters of ancient fame to all comers"* (water had been cut off in 1941 as it was contaminated). Sadly, no water flows today although the well was further restored in the restoration scheme.

Kemp's original plans for the park included a refreshment pavilion. This was designed by the Borough Surveyor, James Bower, working to Kemp's plans, and was eventually built in 1881. The building took longer than the Park Committee anticipated but the contractor, Mr Clarke explained that the delay was due *"to the very long winter I had – [I] had the whole of the brickwork and stone work to repoint from frost. I will … have it fit for occupation by June 1st."*

Known today as the Almond Pavilion, the building takes its name from Mr G.E. Almond, a wallpaper merchant, who donated the clock in 1903 to celebrate his business's jubilee.

Originally added to the side of the pavilion's west front, this spoilt Kemp's octagonal shape and when the pavilion was restored, the clock was replaced flat on the west front.

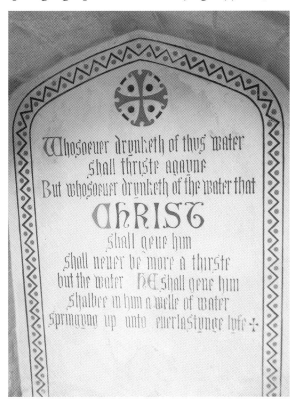

The Salte Welle inscription.

The first tenant was a Mr Cawthorne who paid an annual rent of £50. He was succeeded by the hapless Mr Bean who within a year, was reported as *"much behind in his tenancy"* and then by Mr Shanley who was allowed occasional use of the Indo-Chinese Pavilion *"at a reasonable cost on temperance principles"*. As had the tenants before him, Mr Shanley repeatedly asked permission to sell refreshments on Sundays but was always refused. He fell foul of the Park Committee in 1892 for serving supper parties in the refreshment house after the park's closing time and was given three months notice to quit as a result. However, this was later rescinded.

It was the next tenant, Mr Sanders, however, who caused the Park Committee the most problems. In 1898, he complained to the Council that he and his family had all been struck down with fever and said *"My doctor blames the drains for all illness"* and asked the Council to pay him compensation as he had spent over £9 in medical fees. The council declined, carried out a cursory inspection of the drains and pronounced themselves satisfied. Three years later however, in autumn 1901, one of Mr Sander's daughters developed scarlet fever which resulted in the refreshment house being closed for nine weeks. This time, the drains were properly inspected, repaired and improved. But relations with the Committee had become strained and when members learnt that Mr Sanders was behind in his rent, they decided they were not satisfied with the way the refreshment house was being run and the County Court Bailiff took possession of it in 1908. Mr Sanders was left both jobless and homeless as tenants of the refreshment house lived 'above the shop'.

The Almond Pavilion.

The most successful tenant, who occupied the Almond Pavilion for a number of years, was Henry Stoddart who took over in 1908. In 1912, when he complained that *"I find it impossible to make the business pay"* and cited the fact that day trippers were now going to Whitley Bay, his annual rent was reduced from £80 to £61. He and his wife made their own ice cream which sold for ¹/₂d a cornet.

The shelter house at the north end of the Broad Walk.

East Lodge – which originally housed the senior servant of the mansion house.

During the 1990s, a series of fires virtually destroyed the Pavilion which was completely rebuilt as part of the subsequent restoration programme. The shelter houses at either end of the Broad Walk were designed by Bower and were modelled on those in Regent's Park, London which the Chelsea-born Bower would have known well. They were added in 1882 and both were restored in 1996.

The two entrance lodges to the park were also designed by Bower. As well as serving a useful purpose for accommodation for park workers and house servants, they also served as a reminder to the casual visitor that the park was manned and that they had entered a special place which demanded certain standards of behaviour.

The earlier of the two is the East Lodge, built in 1881 by Greason & Stockdale for £378 5s 10d (£378.29). Unfortunately when the Park Sub-committee carried out an initial inspection of this building they found that *"all of the work appeared to be unsatisfactory in workmanship"* and the firm were ordered to improve. Bower designed the East Lodge in a style sympathetic to Saltwell Towers using the same decorative brickwork. However, whilst very pretty externally, it had no indoor toilet until 1965!

The Dene Lodge, designed with two rooms and two attics, was built in 1886 and was, for many years, occupied by the park's resident policeman. The tenancy was first offered to the Watch Committee in May 1887 at a rent of 5/- (25p) per week, on condition that the wife of the officer attend to the entrance gates. The lodge was carefully situated, and with a degree of forward planning, so that it would be unaffected should Saltwell Lane later be improved (which it was in the 1930s).

The park keeper's house was originally a single storey building. A top floor was added in 1893, an additional bedroom and bathroom were added in 1904 and electricity was installed in 1931. Other practical buildings for the park included the propagating houses, the first of which was added in 1897 and purchased from Richardson & Co of Darlington. This was 30 feet long, 14 feet wide and cost £34 10s 2d (£34.51).

The stable block, requested by Hugh Clayton Armstrong in 1881, was sympathetically designed by James Bower to complement the

Dene Lodge and its lovely gates.

polychromatic style of the mansion house. Mounted on its gable end is the park bell which, for many years, was the signal that the park was about to close. The hapless loiterer who ignored the warnings of the bell was then faced with an ignominious climb over the park railings. The coach house alongside was built at the same time.

Park House – home to the Park Superintendent.

The stable designed by James Bower with the park bell to the left.

Avenue Green Bowling Pavilion.

There have been a variety of bowling pavilions within the park over the years. The current Avenue Green Bowling Pavilion was an import from the North East Coast Exhibition, held on the Town Moor, Newcastle, in 1929. A new pavilion, the George Wilkes Bowling Pavilion (named after the donor, a well known Gateshead shop owner, *see advert page 18*) was designed by A. Leslie Berry, Gateshead Council's chief architect and opened in 1963. George Wilkes also provided money for a ladies' bowling pavilion which was eventually opened in 1970 after a dispute with Wilkes, who originally wanted admission limited to members of the Saltwell Ladies Bowling Club only. Described as sun lounges, neither building was really warm enough and both buildings were demolished as part of the restoration plan. (*See photo right.*)

George Wilkes Pavilion.

The most exotic building ever to have appeared in the park was, without doubt, the Indo-Chinese Pavilion. This was purchased in 1887 for £50 for the park to use as an additional refreshment pavilion. It had been designed by an American architect, J.S. Fairfax, for Lyon's tea and coffee company to serve as their tea house at the Newcastle Jubilee Exhibition, on Newcastle's Town Moor, in 1887 where it was described as *"light and elegant … externally decorated in the Indian style and combined appearance of domes and minarets, with a profusion of bright colours, produces a very fine effect"*. As such it was the pre-cursor to Lyon's cafés which became known as Lyon's Corner Houses. The cost of removal and re-erection in the park came to a little over £150 and was considered money well spent at the time.

The Indo-Chinese Pavilion – The park's most exotic building.

A bowling match takes place against a backdrop of the Indo-Chinese Pavilion.

However, the pavilion had only been designed as a temporary building and, like the mansion house, looked better from the outside than on the inside. This can be seen in a request to use it from the Dunelm Orchestra of Low Fell in 1912, which ended *"providing the place is made presentable"*.

Although it remained a fixture in the park for the next seventy years, it was never the success it could have been and was invariably described as in a poor or even dilapidated condition. It was occasionally opened for the sale of teas and other refreshments in the park but Mr Stoddart, who ran the Almond Pavilion for a number of years, complained that food could not be kept overnight in the Indo-Chinese Pavilion due to rats. The building had a number of alternative uses – at one time it stored the yachts for the Model Yacht Club and during the First World War, was used as an armoury by the Gateshead Volunteer Training Corps. In winter, it housed the boats used on the lake during the summer season.

The original wooden boat attendant's hut.

Eventually, by the 1950s the building was in poor condition with the council facing a dilemma of complete refurbishment or replacement. Although it was given a lick of paint in 1951, its days were numbered and it was finally demolished in 1958. It was replaced by a new café which opened in May of the same year – a rather less attractive building now known as the Training Centre. In an attempt to attract a younger audience, a jukebox was installed in 1963. However, this was not enough to raise profits and by 1966, the café was only being used for special occasions or for private hire.

And its brick built replacement.

The Council bought other buildings from the 1887 exhibition – as well as the Pavilion, four small buildings were bought for £10 and a newspaper kiosk for a further £10. One of these buildings was used as a ticket office for the boats on the lake. This was made of wood but was described as dilapidated in 1921 and was replaced by a new office of brick.

Of course for many people, the most essential buildings were the lavatories. First installed in May 1876, ready for the park's opening, they originally included a mix of earth closets and WCs and were usually situated beside the recreational areas. Toilets and urinals were frequently considered by the Park Committee with recurring requests noted to *"look at provision"* and one very firm request to the Park Superintendent in 1888 to account for their very poor state. Usually, these were erected by Gateshead firms but in October 1880, the Chalet Company applied for permission to erect what was rather coyly termed a 'Chalet de necessité' and public lavatories. Admission was one penny to use the retiring room with an extra penny charged for the use of the lavatory. The Council agreed, but only on the understanding that their own toilets remain free.

In 1909, all the WCs were condemned as they did not meet the Water Company's standards and all had to have new metal cisterns installed. Gradually over the years, the old primitive lavatories were removed and replaced and then, in 1979, came the arrival of the 'superloos'. This building, (still used in a reduced form today) contained ladies and gents toilets together with rest rooms. The cost was £48,000.

Behind the toilets in the south west corner of the playground was a small 'first aid' room. However, this seems to have been distinctly short of facilities – in 1927, it was recorded that there was no running water, wash basin, electric light, radiator or electric kettle!

Over the years, the park has been the scene of continuing building development. However, not all proposals have been adopted. When the town centre was being re-developed in the mid 1960s, Holy Trinity Church on the High Street was under threat of demolition and there was a proposal to re-erect it in Saltwell Park. Thankfully, that never happened.

Gates were a necessary feature of the park and Kemp's purpose built park entrance at the Avenue Road entrance has gates produced by the Gateshead firm of Bainbridge & Crimson, which show Gateshead's original

The Art Nouveau gates at the entrance opposite Saltwell Cemetery.

Coat of Arms, alongside the date of 1876 – the date the park opened. The same firm produced the ornamental gates beside the entrance to the Dene (*see advert on page 7*). These ornate, Art Nouveau style gates were awarded a bronze medal at the Paris International Exposition in 1878 and were offered to the park in 1885 for £25. The gates, with their pillars, designed by the same firm were originally an extension of the Salte Welle wall, as can be seen by the photograph bottom left. However, when Saltwell Road South was constructed in the 1930s, these gates were moved and are now slightly north west of their original location as can be seen in the photograph bottom right.

Other gates in the park have been added at various times including the replacement gates at the Brinkburn Avenue entrance to the park which were constructed in 1982 to replace *"battered and rusty wrought iron gates"*. They were made by teenagers on a Youth Opportunities Programme working with British Shipbuilders in Middlesbrough.

The Salte Welle as Wailes created it.

Image from the 1930s showing the truncated wall.

There are 12 Grade II listed buildings in Saltwell Park. These have been listed by English Heritage as nationally important and of special interest. They are:

Belvedere walls, turrets and staircases, 1860s
Saltwell Towers, c 1871
George Charlton drinking fountain, 1876
The Broad Walk, 1877
Aviaries (2), 1880
Stable block, 1881
Park House, c 1881
North and South shelters on the Broad Walk, 1882
Alderman Lucas statue, 1903
South African War Memorial, 1905

Memorials and Statues

Memorials and statues have been a feature of the park from the beginning. In April 1876, even before the park opened to the public, the Gateshead Observer was reporting a proposal to erect a drinking fountain. Kemp had planned this as one of the park's features and on 5 September 1876, the gothic style stone and granite fountain was unveiled by Robert Spence Watson, a noted local Liberal and Quaker reformer and philanthropist. It was dedicated to George Charlton (1808-85), a butcher, Mayor in 1874-75 and a noted Primitive Methodist preacher. Charlton was a strong temperance man (the drinking fountain was, therefore, a very appropriate memorial to him) who had strongly supported the idea of the park, although he had a constant running battle with the Chief Constable John Elliott over Elliott's various proposals to provide animals and birds for the park.

A bust of George Charlton is shown on the front of the fountain together with Gateshead's then Coat of Arms and an inscription *"GEORGE CHARLTON ESQ JP Mayor of Gateshead 1874 and 1875 in recognition of his labours in the cause of social reform"*. The fountain is one of the park's twelve Grade II listed structures.

There is only one actual statue in the park and that shows Alderman John Lucas in his Mayoral robes and is situated on the Broad Walk. John Lucas, a firebrick manufacturer of Carlton Terrace, Low Fell, was a noted Liberal, a strong educationalist, a pioneer of the mechanics' institute and also took a prominent part in the works of the River Tyne Commission. He served on Gateshead Council for many years and was Mayor between 1888-90.

The George Charlton memorial fountain.

Like the drinking fountain, this memorial is also Grade II listed. Eleven feet high and constructed of bronze, the statue was designed by W. Grant Stevenson RSA of Edinburgh. J.G. Hodgson, a Newcastle quarry owner, provided the stone for the plinth. Originally intended to be erected on West Street in the town centre, it was unveiled on Saturday 9 May 1903 by Ald. Thomas Richardson of Newcastle who was, like Lucas himself, a keen educationalist. Richardson was a hasty substitute for Earl Grey who sent a telegram on the day of the unveiling saying he was indisposed.

John Lucas, Mayor of Gateshead.

There are three distinct war memorials in Saltwell Park although only two are in conventional form. The third and most recent is the timber bridge which was rebuilt as part of the 1998 restoration and is dedicated to men of the 6th, 8th and 9th Battalions of the Durham Light Infantry who fought in Sicily during Second World War. In July 1943, they held the Primosole Bridge, a site of strategic importance, as part of Operation Fustian. Prior to the restoration, the men were commemorated with a metal plaque fixed to the exterior of one of the belvedere walls. The bridge replaces an earlier stone bridge and spans Wailes' ha-ha.

It was proposed to erect a monument to the South African War in January 1904. Various sites were discussed but it was eventually decided that it should be situated to the south of the mansion and a new footpath was built to connect the memorial to the bridge.

The memorial was formally unveiled by Sir John French, a veteran of the Boer War, on Saturday 11 November 1905 (a date which, a few years later, would become particularly memorable) at 3.30pm before thousands of spectators. These included widows of men who had died in the war and surviving soldiers (who could only attend if they wore their medals). 1,000 troops were on parade.

Of the 900 Gateshead men who served in the Boer War, 77 never returned. These men are recorded on the memorial, which has a bronze figure of Peace, sculpted by Francis W. Doyle Jones, on top of a granite pedestal. The inscription, taken from a poem by the noted eighteenth century poet William Collins reads:

The Primosole Bridge with details of the Sicilian campaign in lettering.

*"How sleep the brave who sink to rest,
By all their country's wishes blest!
By fairy hands their knell is rung
By forms unseen their dirge is sung!"*

There is one other war memorial in Saltwell Park. It was unveiled in July 1981 by the Mayor of Newcastle and is a memorial to 1,419 officers & men of the Durham Light Infantry who were killed in action between 1900-45. This is a sandstone wall containing three memorial plaques headed the 5th Durham Rifle Volunteers (which later became the 9th Battalion of the DLI, known as the Gateshead battalion). On the left hand plaque is inscribed:
"In memory of 1419 officers and other ranks who laid down their lives in war from 1900-1945 each a son of the 9th Battalion the Durham Light Infantry T.A. Faithful". ('The Faithful Durhams' is a nickname of the DLI dating back to 1772.)

The right hand plaque records: *"These stones were*

The South African War Memorial with the statue of Peace.

The DLI Memorial

recovered from the Drill Hall in Burt Terrace [Gateshead] *home of the 9th Battalion the Durham Light Infantry TA dedicated AD July 1981".* In front of the wall are two specially designed seats which each display the DLI badge. The memorial replaces one which was formerly in St Mary's Church, Gateshead but was destroyed by fire in 1979.

Another memorial, which was temporary but no less memorable, was the hosting of the British Legion's first regional Field of Remembrance in the park which opened for a few weeks on 28 October 2012. Over 10,000 small wooden crosses were placed at the approach to the South African War Memorial as a tribute to soldiers from Gateshead who lost their lives in conflict.

There is only one Blue Plaque in the park. This celebrates William Wailes and was erected in 2005 outside the north entrance to Saltwell Towers. William Wailes was born in 1808 and spent his early life in Bearl in the Tyne Valley, Northumberland. He established a grocery business in Mosley Street, Newcastle in 1830 but within 10 years had begun to manufacture stained glass. Some of his earliest, and best work, was produced for A.W.N. Pugin (the country's pre-eminent Roman Catholic architect) and his windows can be found in churches and cathedrals throughout the British Isles. At its peak, his factory was producing almost one new church window every day. This very successful business gave Wailes the money to buy his estate and create his 'no expense spared' house.

The local Pre-Raphaelite artist William Bell Scott described William Wailes as *"a genial man of moderate height, very stout, with one of the happiest faces in creation"*.

Above: The bronze statue of Peace stands in solitary splendour in Saltwell Park.

Left: A worthy remembrance of a hard working man.

The final memorial in the park is situated at the entrance to the Rose Garden. This commemorates workers who have lost their life through their work. The present memorial was unveiled in 2010 and replaced an earlier memorial erected in 1998. An annual service is held here on Workers Memorial Day on 28 April.

Right: The Workers Memorial Plaque.

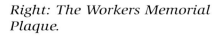

Entertainment

Music has always been a feature of the park with performances taking place over time from three different bandstands, one stage-cum-kiosk and six different locations! There have been a variety of bands including that of the Abbot Memorial School who played in the park from 6pm until 8pm on Sundays and were given an annual grant of five guineas for *"their services during summer nights"*.

Although Sunday concerts have always featured in the park, they have often been the subject of controversy. Once concerts began, there were frequent complaints that the music played was of a secular rather than a sacred nature and in 1902, on two separate occasions, members of both the Free Church Council and the High Street Wesleyan Circuit made formal complaints which resulted in a directive to conductors of bands booked to play in the park on Sundays that they should not include anything in their programme *"which might be calculated to offend anyone"*. It was subsequently agreed that the Park Committee should censor the music although this decision also caused complaints and the Committee was accused of being too dictatorial.

The first concerts were free but collections were usually allowed. Sometimes however, the collectors themselves were a little too over zealous as can be seen from this comment; *"those who take collections for the bands … on Sundays are too eager to bring to the notice of visitors the voluntary offering box"*. Fetes were often held by the Council to provide money for musical performances in the park and in other locations in Gateshead.

The first bandstand was erected shortly after the park opened in 1876 and seems to have been situated west of where the South African War Memorial is today. It was certainly near enough to the house to have troubled Hugh Clayton Armstrong, who, during his tenancy of Saltwell Towers, asked for the bandstand to be moved to *"a portion of the park more remote from his house"* and offered to pay for its removal.

In August 1893 the Borough Surveyor reported that the roof of the bandstand was in an *"advanced state of decay"* and it was eventually decided that the whole bandstand was rotten and had to be replaced. The replacement bandstand was built by the Glasgow firm of Walter McFarlane and Co (a firm noted for bandstands and drinking

The McFarlane bandstand of 1894.

fountains) at a cost of £142 plus an extra £26 5s (£26.25) to install gas pipes. This was erected on the northern fields in line with the refreshment house and ceremoniously unveiled on 20 June 1894 with a fete and music performed by the Newcastle Military Band.

Performances seem to have been popular, although not necessarily with the musically minded of Gateshead as, within two months of the opening, the policemen on duty were instructed *"to prevent rough play around the bandstand whilst music is being performed"*.

In 1906, 300 wooden folding chairs were bought and placed in an enclosed area around the bandstand. These cost 1d to hire (*see ticket left*) but weren't always needed, as in 1909 when the weather was terrible and in consequence the season had been *"a complete financial failure"*. Much later, in 1950, the chairs were replaced with deckchairs which cost 6d (2½p) to hire. Many people however, preferred the old folding chairs.

Also in 1906, wooden shutters were ordered for the bandstand to protect the players in windy weather. An asphalted path had been created around the bandstand – largely funded from the money received during the concerts. Unfortunately, people preferred to walk on the grass which became so badly damaged that in 1909, the bandstand was moved to the lake. This meant, of course, that the musicians and their

2156

SALTWELL PARK.

CHAIRS

1d.

All tickets must be taken from the Roll, and are issued subject to the Park Bye-Laws and examination by the Park Superintendent.

1d for a folding chair in 1906.

instruments now had to be transported to the island. The move was not popular, either with the performers or with the public, and complaints were frequent. One of the first complaints received was a letter from the Labour Representation Committee in 1910 who complained *"the performers were so far removed from the audience as to render many of the finest passages in the music inaudible"*. The committee also complained of *"the animal spirits and noise"* of some of the younger people

Bandsmen performing on the island with their boats moored alongside.

who attended. When Felling Colliery Band were booked to play in the same year, they asked if they could bring their own bandstand with them and were reported as saying *"I think everybody seems tired of the band on the lake"*. In 1913, the St Hilda Colliery Band from South Shields wrote to the Park Committee saying they were willing to play but only on the bandstand in its old position. They were even willing to give 10% of the proceeds to the Gateshead Dispensary if this was done, but to no avail – the bandstand remained where it was and the band did not play. In 1919, when the 1st Battalion of the Seaforth Highlanders played, a local newspaper reported *"The items were at times not heard to full advantage on account of the wind which blew in strong and frequent gusts"*.

The bandstand was eventually moved into the Grove extension when that opened in 1921. This bandstand, one of the few McFarlane bandstands to survive the Second World War cull of railings, was dismantled in 1976 and moved to Beamish Museum where it can be seen close to another Gateshead artefact – Ravensworth Terrace. Its replacement was a rather less attractive stage-cum-kiosk nearer to the lake nicknamed 'The Cube', on the site of the old 'ocean wave' (a 1920s piece of play apparatus). This was itself replaced in 1991 by a bandstand from Bishop Auckland and returned to a new site in the Grove. This bandstand was first seen in Gateshead at the National Garden Festival. It was loaned by Beamish Museum who agreed a permanent loan to the Council once the Festival had finished.

'The Cube'.

The most frequent performers in the park have been brass bands and some highly prestigious bands have played here. However, these often came at a price as, for example, when the Black Dyke Mills Band played in 1956. They were paid £72 at a time when most bands were receiving on average, about £14 to perform.

When attendances began to decline in the 1960s, the Council looked for new ways to provide music. The River City Jazzmen gave a successful performance in 1961 which led to them being asked back the following season and a note in the Council Minutes records that more jazz bands were asked to play. Pop music was also discussed but the first pop group was paid off after an hour and other groups would not consider performing for the low fee they were being offered.

It was not just the bands and the bandstands however, that provided music in the park. In 1902, for the Coronation Fete, a male voice choir performed in the rowing boats on the lake. Music from the

Once in Bishop Auckland, this is what bands in Saltwell Park use today

roundabouts, which often appeared in the summer seasons in the parks, was sometimes a cause for complaint as in this instance *"… the incessant grinding of the organ from 2.30 to 10 must indeed be a nerve-racking ordeal"*. In 1953, householders in nearby Saltwell View threatened the Council with legal action when they discovered that, after three years of peace, the roundabouts would be returning, with hurdy gurdies and a steam organ to provide the music.

A celebrated group of local performers, Will Bradley's minstrels, gave a performance in 1901 in the then playground area at the north west corner of the park. They paved the way for pierrot troupes which first appeared in the park in 1903 courtesy of Mr H. Broomfield and his 'Paragon Concert Party'. However, these troupes were never a very regular feature in the park and were frequently refused permission to perform by the Council. One of the most celebrated groups was Will Knowles 'Domino Set Entertainers' who performed for the first time in the park in the Grove on 20 July 1921 and were invited back on other occasions.

In 1951, the Osiris Repertory Company of Worcester, gave open air performances as part of the Saltwell Park Show and as part of their Festival of Britain tour. Formed during the Second World War to provide high class entertainment, they were an all female group who specialised in performances of Shakespearean plays.

Other entertainment was more homegrown. In May 1937, Gateshead Amateur Operatic Society gave a performance of Merrie England in the park as part of the Coronation festivities for George VI (*see photograph below*). This light opera was performed again in the park during the 1953 Coronation festivities. On that occasion, bad weather meant that some performances had to be held in the town hall.

High class entertainment in the park from the Osiris Repertory Company.

Recreation

The park is an obvious place for games and sports but originally not all sports were encouraged. In July 1877, the Secretary of the North Durham Cricket ground asked permission to use the four northern fields for football. The application was considered by the Park Committee who recorded rather summarily that the request *"be not entertained"* and it was to be many years before ball games were allowed in the park. A similar request by the Collingwood Cricket Club in 1886 to lease a portion of one of the fields was also refused.

The game of bowls however, which was one of Kemp's planned features, was an early sport in the park and the first bowling green (complete with turf removed from the site of Sheriff Hill Fever Hospital) opened in 1878. Four pairs of bowls were bought in 1879 and it was agreed regulations for use should be based on those already in existence in Leazes Park, Newcastle. Like many of the early structures in the park, perhaps taking inspiration from Wailes' turrets, this green was octagonal – a very unusual shape for a bowling green. It was an immediate success, business was brisk and within a few years there were numerous requests for another green. In 1887,

Octagonal bowling green.

Saltwell Park's second bowling green was built near the lake beside the new tennis courts.

This new green proved equally popular and a third was opened in July 1901, with the Mayoral garden party held in the Indo-Chinese Pavilion to celebrate the event. This green was the largest in the park and was 47 yards square. It was, and still is, the most impressive with its sloping sides and ornamental stairs and cost £385. It was constructed by Tom Smith of Hawick who was regarded as an expert on the construction of bowling greens.

Bowls match in progress on the park's 1901 bowling green with the Indo-Chinese Pavilion in the background.

In 1910, a visitor to the park was impressed to discover yet another bowling green was in the course of construction and wrote *"A new green was just receiving its finishing touches when I was at Saltwell and I should suppose that so far at least as the turf laying is concerned it is by this time completed. It is a fine healthy game suitable for young, old and middle aged and scores of men were busily engaged in it on the other beautiful greens on the day of my visit".*

Work on this green was largely done by unskilled labour – men who were selected by the Distress Committee – and the contract was awarded to a Mr Provan of Rutherglen at £305 18s 3d (£305.92). Today, this green has a very attractive small bowling pavilion known as the Avenue Green Pavilion (*see page 29*).

Charges were reasonable – in 1892 it cost 1d per person per hour. However, in 1913, the Saltwell Park Bowling Club (who had by now divided into two groups, the other being the Gateshead Borough Bowling Club) complained to the Park Committee requesting a reduction in costs as they considered they were paying 50% more than other clubs. The secretary wrote *"it is a game which has made rapid strides in recent years, and when one comes to consider the benefits accruing from a social and moral standpoint, it is really in the interest of the town itself for the Council to foster the game and allow its townsmen the privilege of playing at the same fee as is charged in Newcastle and other neighbouring towns".*

In an attempt to preserve the turf of the greens, it was decided that new regulations regarding footwear were needed, so overshoes were ordered in 1901 and hired at 1d per pair.

During the 1930s there were frequent proposals to replace the old octagonal green but despite being regarded by the Council as *"very old with many faults"*, it continued to be used and in the Second World War, permission was granted to the 'Old Men's Club' to use it on weekdays from 1pm – 5pm for 1d each per hour (the same charge as in 1892!).

By 1939, the park had no less than six bowling greens – double the number it has today. Two further greens were situated next to the present day tennis courts. When one of these bowling greens was completely destroyed by fire in late 1996 the fire service had to pump water from the lake due to the low pressure of the water supply.

The Mayor, Coun Pickering with Gateshead's MP Tom Magnay, to the right, at a bowls tournament in 1939.

Councillor Silas Kent had proposed a quoit ground for the park in 1885 but it was another three years before this appeared next to the second bowling green. It remained a feature in the park until 1928 when it was transformed into a small bowling green for juniors.

Concentration on the putting green.

This shows a match between the Mayor of Gateshead using the black draughts and the Mayor of South Shields in c 1938.

A putting green was added in 1922 and was situated beside the Maze. By the 1950s there were also six open air draughts boards.

Gymnastics were an earlier feature of the park with the first equipment appearing in 1897 – the forerunner of today's 'green gym' which can be found beside the tennis courts.

Tennis was another early sport, and tennis courts were, like the octagonal bowling green, featured in Kemp's plan for the park. Courts were set out south of the lake in 1885 – unfortunately no one had thought to order either nets or racquets, an omission which had to be speedily rectified! These first courts were situated on the area today used for the under eight's playground.

In 1923, two sets of courts were established. The first set was on what today is the over eight's play area, whilst the other courts are those which are in use today near the north east of the lake. These courts and the older 1885 courts were all given new 'grassphalte' (a new improved sports surface) surfaces, manufactured by the En-Tout-Cas Company.

Fashions in tennis wear for ladies changed over the years which had consequences for the first two young women who were spotted wearing tennis skirts in 1919 and reported to the Park Superintendent for indecency! Along with many other sports in the park however, tennis was forbidden on Sundays and even a letter from the Public Parks Lawn Tennis Association in 1922 requesting that all parks allow tennis to be played on Sundays had no effect. Eventually the rule was relaxed but even until well into the twentieth century, ball

All courts in play.

games were only allowed to be played on Sundays during the summer season. In 1906, the fine for ignoring this ruling was a staggering 40 shillings (£2).

The lake was, and still is, a very popular recreation area. Once it was formed, it was frequently used for skating which became an entertaining seasonal pastime during the park's early years. Skating proved to be a lucrative venture for the Council and eight days skating in the months of December 1885 and January 1886 netted the council a profit of £80 16s (£80.80). This money was frequently used to pay for new paths to be formed in various areas throughout the park and also as donations to the Gateshead District Relief Fund.

Boys in the 1940s having fun on the frozen paddling pool.

Today's model boats out on the lake.

The lake was also used by the Model Yacht Club founded in 1886, and its successor, the Model Boat Club (founded in 2002), still use it today. Arthur Newall, who lived at nearby Ferndene and was secretary of the Yacht Club in its early days, conducted a war against rowing boats on the lake and made frequent requests for the use of a boat to rescue the club's 'wrecked boats' on the island. These requests, along with his other requests for the Council to cut back, or allow yacht club members to cut back, foliage on the island which was interfering with model craft were constantly refused and became a source of aggravation to the club. However, when in 1904, the Model Yacht Club presented a petition to the council requesting that the lake needed clearing as it was full of rubbish, and barbed wire fencing in some areas made it impossible to retrieve vessels *"In consequence of pleasure boats being rowed by incompetent persons who recklessly collide with each other many valuable yachts have been damaged"* they were eventually allowed to buy a boat to retrieve their yachts, for which they then had to pay an annual fee.

Rowing boats were bought by the council in 1882, shortly after the lake had been made, the Local Government Board having refused the council permission to lease them. New boats were added over the years, including four boats supplied by Palmers shipyards in Jarrow for £10 in 1896. By this time there were 20 boats operating on the lake. At first when boats were hired, tickets had to be laboriously written out by the attendant although pre-printed tickets appeared in 1898. Not everyone abided by the rules however, and in 1894 it was realised that some people were picking up extra passengers out of sight of the attendant at the boat house. Notices were erected around the lake warning that 'illegal' passengers would be charged double fare. It wasn't always easy being in charge of the boats – a statement which Mr Wheatley, the boat attendant might have agreed with in 1919 when he was assaulted by an unhappy customer.

The canoeist in this photograph is obviously quite proficient.

One vessel, not quite so successful as the rowing boats, was the canoe which, in May 1891 was reported, *"had already capsized thrice".* This perhaps reflects more on the ability of the canoeist than on the actual canoe!

In June 1909 a motor boat, the 'John Maccoy', designed to take 20 people and constructed by boat builder John Rodgers of Cardiff, made its first appearance on the lake. Named after Gateshead's Mayor, John Maccoy, who had pressed for it to be bought, it was certainly successful. In its first month it carried 24,151 passengers with takings of £100 12s 7d (£100.63) and there were reports of 100 yard long queues of people waiting for it. As the boat cost £68, it had already made its money. However, success came at a cost and the engine had to be replaced within a matter of months. The boat was eventually replaced by a new one from W. Hill, shipbuilders of Tyne Dock, South Shields at a cost of £155 although for a time, both boats operated on the lake.

Queues wait patiently for the 'John Maccoy'.

These were not the only motorised boats which appeared on the lake. In 1985, the 'Saltwell Belle' made its first appearance. This was a replica Mississippi steam boat built by apprentices of British Shipbuilders training centre at Hebburn which was driven by petrol, though a paddle wheel was fixed at the rear.

A paddling pool was eventually added to the lake in 1925, having first been proposed as a special project for unemployed men in 1909. Also added was a contraption known as the 'ocean wave' – a piece of equipment which had nothing at all to do with water and was situated near to the swings.

When the lake was first cleared in February 1933 and all the water was

A full load for the motor boat!

drained off, the local press reported *"The results of the great clean up will be ample compensation to those youngsters who have had to forego the joys of the paddling pool".* The pool, always popular with generations of children, was eventually removed due to health and safety reasons in the 1970s.

Children have always had at least one play area in the park. The first proper playground was situated in the north west corner of the park on the site of a small quarry. It was first proposed in 1895 when the Council intended to erect a flat surface play area for marbles, skipping and ball play, whilst underneath would be an underground shooting gallery and skittles alley for adults. It was also proposed that in the winter, the surface could be flooded and used for ice skating. However, this potentially interesting construction was never built.

"There is no bathing pool yet in Northern England which affords such unending recreation to children as does the pool by the side of the lake at Saltwell Park".

The new swings in use in 1920.

The new slide being well used in the 1930s.

Children's swings were erected between the Almond Pavilion and the lake and were well used, as can be seen in the photograph left. They were installed in 1920 with extra swings being brought from Tynevale recreation ground in 1945. These were augmented with two see-saws in 1923. However, as with ball games, using the swings and other play equipment was banned on Sundays for many years.

This picture left shows children enjoying themselves on the new slide which had been bought by the Council in 1931. This was made of steel with a birch sliding surface and cost £35.

In the 1970s the site of the octagonal bowling green was converted into a playground for younger children and today there are two separate adjoining sites for children of different ages, close to the lake and near to where they were originally.

Below: A new use for the octagonal bowling green in the 1970s.

Animals, Birds and Fish

Some of the first animals to be seen in the park were not owned by the Council but by a Mr Hall of Gosforth Hall Farm who, in 1877, paid for the privilege of housing 77 sheep at 5d (2p) per head per week in the northern fields. This was not just a money-making venture on behalf of the Council as the sheep acted as living lawn mowers and by grazing, reduced the need to cut the grass so frequently. Originally, wooden hurdles separated the sheep from the Broad Walk but nothing really separated them from the children's play area beside the lake and there was a complaint in 1906 that the sheep were grazing in the playground.

In the early days, the park also had horses and ponies for practical purposes. One horse was employed in pulling the grass cutter – and had to wear leather boots! As these animals died or became too old for work, they were replaced, as in 1900 when an old pony, unfit for further work, was sold for £2.10s (£2.50) and a new one was bought for £8 10s (£8.50). However, one pony, on loan from another council department during the First World War, had to be returned as it was considered too fast! Normally these working animals were purchased but, in response to the death of a cob in the park in 1905, Alderman Walter Willson offered a 'very sprightly' mare in foal but only on the condition that he could have the foal when it was born.

William Wailes had created two small duck ponds – one at the entrance to the Dene beside Saltwell Lane, the other at the south east corner of the park near the Grove. In February 1877, these were cleaned out, cemented and stocked with ducks and swans presented by a number of donors including the Earl of Ravensworth, Mr Lange (of Heathfield House) and Mr Elliott, the Chief Constable who was always looking for ways to add to the park's wildlife. This set the scene for donations of further birds and animals – in fact virtually all the livestock in the park has been donated rather than bought. At times, the scale of donations was enthusiastic to say the least, and it frequently happened

The ducks in 1939.

that the park found itself with a surfeit of wildlife. Within five months of the restored duck ponds being stocked with these donated birds, the ducks were breeding so well that there was a very sharp increase in numbers with the result that many were sold with two young ducks being offered to each gentleman who had donated ducks earlier. Over the next twenty years, there were regular sales of ducks and swans as for example in 1886 when one sale raised £6 17s 6d (£6.87).

The days of the duck ponds however, were numbered and within a few years of the lake being formed they were removed. In actual fact, there was a construction fault as both ponds constantly leaked.

Within a year of the opening of the park, it was well stocked with bird life and a full list in the Park Committee minutes in 1877 shows 3 swans, 47 ducks, 4 peacocks, 1 peahen, 8 pheasants, 3 hens, 1 bantam cock and 1 bantam hen. The birds were always

Canada geese – some of the lake's noisiest inhabitants today.

popular, so much so that the Dicky Bird Society (all of whose members were children) began an early conservation project in the park when they were involved in creating a number of bird boxes in the park in 1880 and again in 1882. In the last couple of years new bird boxes have been added to the park.

One of the original aviaries of 1880.

As already mentioned, one of the most frequent donors of wildlife was Gateshead's Chief Constable, John Elliott and in August 1877 he made an unsuccessful application to use the strawberry bed at the park for a new pheasantry. Another pheasantry, presented by Lord Northbourne already existed. Not to be deterred, however, he instructed the Gateshead Police Band to give some concerts – the proceeds were then used to erect a new pheasantry at a cost of £50. Two further Amherst pheasants were given in 1911 by another of Gateshead's Mayors,

Lancelot Tulip Penman, with two golden pheasants being donated in 1928 from Mr H.C. Embleton of Nest House, Felling.

Money from further concerts by the Police Band provided enough revenue to pay for two cast iron aviaries in 1880 *"for the reception of singing and other birds"* at a cost of £74. The Council were really powerless to refuse such gifts but may have wished that John Elliott was not quite so persistent in his endeavours. Nevertheless, they wrote *"already a number of valuable birds have been collected and the Committee believe that this collection of birds will be so added to from time to time as to form an increasing object of interest at Saltwell Park".*

It was the monkeys however, that caused the biggest cause of aggravation. In 1880, the Council refused an application by Elliott to raise funds to erect a monkey house. However, once again, they were forced to accept when he raised his own funds, purchased three monkeys at £1 each, a variety of birds including a paroquet (parakeet), canaries, yellow hammer and siskin and provided a monkey house. The house was erected by Bainbridge & Crimson at a cost of £62 7s 1d (£62.36).

Calls for the monkeys to be dispensed with were not long in coming, particularly as their degrees of affection towards each other, often in full view of the public, were not always appreciated and in October 1880 the Park Committee resolved that the male monkeys in the park should be removed. A further motion that the female monkeys be removed forthwith was then taken and until this decision could be ratified by the Council it was decided that *"the monkeys be closed within their house on Sundays"*. However, the female monkeys were subsequently given a reprieve and allowed to stay. A further offer of a monkey from a Mr W.S. Blacklock in 1895 was refused and by the beginning of the twentieth century, the monkeys of Saltwell Park were no more.

But it was not just the monkeys the

Geordies visit to Gyetside Park

The first verse of a poem written by J. Telford described some of the birds in the park c 1880:

Last Tuesday neet aa tewyk a waak

Sometime afore twas dark, man,

Alang the Durham road a bit,

An doon to Geytside Park, man.

Aa cuddent scarce believe ma eyes,

Aa met wi sie a gran' sorprise –

Bords o' various shape an' size,

Wi' a' thor diff'rent shoots an' cries;

Peacocks, bubblyjocks, an' owls,

Torkeys, craws, an' other fowls,

Pigeons, swans, seagulls, an' geese,

Ducks, doves, an' ivvorything te please –

Ye'll fin' at Geytside Park, man.

Fal the dal, the dal, & c.

Council wanted to dispose of. One of the most bizarre additions to the park was removed in 1881 when it was decided to dispose of some ducks and geese *"and also the jackal"*. And dogs too, seemed to be a problem as in 1878 when the Park Committee agreed that wire netting should *"be fixed at those parts of the park boundaries at which dogs are in the habit of entering from the adjoining fields"*.

An owl (this may have been an eagle owl donated by John Elliott) also came under threat in January 1885 although it did, at least, receive a temporary stay of execution when, although *"The Committee had under consideration the condition of the owl at the park as to whether sufficient amusement was obtained therefrom to compensate of the cost of its keep"* it was decided to keep it over the winter.

A racoon was offered to London Zoo in 1891, after which it was resolved that *"in future no vicious animal be allowed to be taken to the park"*. This was probably a very wise decision as two years earlier the council had been forced to pay £650 (approximately £650,000 today) compensation when George Townsend, a young man from Granville Street near the Park, was gored by a stag which had escaped its enclosure. Grazing beside the bandstand on the northern fields, it spied George as he walked along the Broad Walk and decided to attack him. George was gored in the left thigh and armpit whilst the stag was subsequently killed as a result of the efforts of passers by trying to help him.

Unsurprisingly, George's solicitor submitted a claim for compensation in which he quoted from George's doctor *"I feel confident that it will be twelve months or more before he will be able to walk comfortably without the aid of stick or crutch and I do not think the leg will ever be as strong or so useful a member as it was before the accident"*.

The response from the council was to request that George be subject to an examination by another doctor, Dr Wilson, and also that *"further information about the antecedents of the stag"* be obtained. The stag probably came with good credentials as it is likely this was one of two deer presented to the park by Lord Ravensworth in 1882. With this as an unfortunate memory, it took the Council no time at all some years later in 1921, to refuse a subsequent offer of a stag from Mr R.F. Fallaw!

One of today's swans.

Two Royal swans arrived in the park during 1903 – a gift of Edward VII. The Park Committee were delighted and recorded *"The Committee report the arrival of two Royal swans both of which are very excellent specimens"*. These birds had had to be specially applied for, unlike the donations of two swans from Mr R.A. Lamb in 1880 and a single swan from William Wears, a butcher on Gateshead High Street in 1900.

During the First World War, the number of birds in the park were allowed to drop in number, largely for economic reasons. Once the war ended, the park was re-stocked with birds and repairs were made to one of the octagonal aviaries which was reported to be in very poor condition. In the 1930s there was a report of about thirty rook nests in the park. However, due to the damage the rooks did to the bowling greens, they were culled on a yearly basis and soon disappeared.

In 1973, an 80 year old cockatoo, nicknamed 'Whitey', on account of its colouring, dropped dead from its perch. It was the end of an era – the park's oldest inhabitant was no more. Such was its fame that the Council decided to have it stuffed. Between its demise and eventual transportation to Doncaster for stuffing, it was important the bird was kept in a state of preservation and not allowed to decay. The Queen Elizabeth Hospital refused to allow it to stay in their morgue so an appeal went out to see if anyone had a spare fridge. Eventually this was successful, after which the bird was stuffed and subsequently presented to the Shipley Gallery where it was given pride of place in the then curator's office.

End of an era

SALTWELL PARK'S oldest inhabitant — an 80-year-old cockatoo — has turned its tail up for good.

The bird, with its white plumage and yellow comb, has been a particular favourite with generations of children.

Parents often brought their youngsters along to point out the bird their mums and grannies took them to see in the past.

An era ended recently when the bird dropped dead from its perch.

The Gateshead Post, 24 May 1973.

Thefts of birds have taken place throughout the park's history. In 1891, a large number of birds were stolen from the island and in 1939, all the budgies save one were stolen from the aviary. Two peacocks were later stolen from their cages which were described as not being strong enough and in 1977, a two year old peacock was found dead on the putting green.

In 1976 there was a report of three wayward birds nicknamed Marty the Magpie, Phil the Pheasant and Pinky the Goose, misbehaving. Marty was stealing eggs, Phil had bitten his keeper, whilst disruptive Pinky had annoyed other birds on the lake. In consequence they were put behind bars in the parks 'top security section' until the end of the breeding season!

Fish were common in the lake but one particular type of fish which made the headlines in the 1980s was the pike. Reports of a monster pike were reported in September 1981 with dawn patrols being set up to catch illegal anglers. The pike was nicknamed 'Jaws' and was supposedly three feet long although the Park Superintendent at first denied its existence. However, following claims that more than 20 ducklings had been devoured, newspaper headlines in June 1982 proclaimed *"Pike doomed to death"*. Death was to be by powder scattered on the lake which was intended to remove oxygen and make the fish come to the surface. However, this didn't work and the fish was eventually caught by more conventional means in March 1984. 'Jaws the killer pike' measuring over three feet long was removed together with 150 other pike, one of which had a live perch still inside which was given to the Hancock Museum. In the attempt to catch the fish, a mechanical digger which had been sent to dig out the mud got stuck and had to be dug out by a second digger!

"Fowl Play in the Park" screamed the headlines in the Gateshead Post of 22 August 1996. The article began *"In the early hours of the morning a family were wrapped in blankets, bundled into a van and driven to the border by a gang of mysterious men"*. This wasn't quite so terrifying as it sounds as it referred to a family of breeding swans who, because the lake was due to be cleared the following week as part of a clean-up operation, were being transported to Berwick.

And finally ...

Saltwell Park is a tribute to the many gardeners who have cared for it. Buildings, events and other features may have come and gone over the years but it is the park itself with its magnificent trees and lovely flower displays which most people enjoy and remark upon. The most successful features are those which support this landscape rather than detract from it and these are the ones we see in the park today.

Designed as the 'green lung' of Victorian Gateshead, the 'People's Park' still serves the same purpose today providing free attractions for people (and dogs!) of all ages.

Edwardian children on the Broad Walk pose as requested for the photographer.

Children in the 1970s enjoying the pedaloes.